how to be
Chaste
while
being Chased

OTHER BOOKS AND TALKS ON CASSETTE
BY CURTIS JACOBS:

The Second Coming: Great or Dreadful?

Stand a Little Taller

I Stand All Amazed

What Girls Wish Guys Knew, and Vice Versa

how to be Chaste while being Chased

Curtis Jacobs

Covenant Communications, Inc.

Covenant

Cover drawing, *Couple on the Run* by Val Chadwick Bagley, Licensed by Curtis Jacobs

Cover design copyrighted 2004 by Covenant Communications, Inc.

Published by Covenant Communications, Inc.
American Fork, Utah

Printed in Canada
First Printing: January 2004

08 07 06 05 04 03 02 01   10 9 8 7 6 5 4 3 2 1

ISBN 1-59156-374-7

TABLE OF CONTENTS

Three Cheers for Chastity

Over the years, as I have taught seminary and institute, I have asked my students a question. I hand each of them a piece of paper and ask them not to include their names with their answers so they can be completely honest. The question is this: "What do you consider to be the three greatest temptations facing youth today?" I collect their papers and tabulate the results. Can you guess what has been the number-one answer each time I have done this? It should be no surprise that year after year the answer is the same—immorality.

President Ezra Taft Benson once said, "The plaguing sin of this generation is sexual immorality. This, the Prophet Joseph Smith said, would be the source of more temptations, more buffetings, and more difficulties for the elders of Israel than any other (see *Journal of Discourses,* 8:55.)" ("Cleansing the Inner Vessel," *Ensign*, May 1986, 4).

Prophets know and have known for centuries how hard it is to keep this law. Over and over they have warned us that it would be a major temptation to break it. Why is immorality one of Satan's most successful tools in his bag of tricks? I ask you to consider one reason you may not have considered.

When I ask my students the question, "Why did we come to earth?" they all chime in with the normal Sunday School answers: "To get a body" or "To be tested." The minute that first answer is thrown out, someone inevitably shouts, "I've been robbed!" But the issue is not whether you want a refund on the body you were given. (You can take that issue up with the complaint department upstairs. Being vertically challenged at 5'7", I have put in a complaint and am waiting for my post-resurrection 6'4" studly redo.) Have you ever considered that one of the most important aspects of the test of mortality is to see who controls our body? Does our spirit control our body, or is it the other way around? Do we let the "natural man" have control (think of the scripture mastery verse Mosiah 3:19), or do we try to yield to the promptings of the Holy Spirit? One of the big questions on the final "mortality exam" will likely be in regards to how we used—or misused—this God-given gift, our body.

We need to remember something about the plan of our Father in Heaven. Lucifer, that great loser, was denied the opportunity to have a body of his own. As a result, he hates those who have one. So if you're human, you're included! Simply put, he just hates all humans. Let me tell you a little story, the parable of the "Pretty Pink Princess Kitchen."

When our three oldest kids were younger, we gave Sarah, our daughter, a Pretty Pink Princess Kitchen, which was made out of thin particle board and painted bright pink. Every girl's dream is to have a bright pink kitchen to slave in, isn't it? She was delighted. However, to her dismay, her two younger brothers liked to put worms, dead birds, and spiders in the oven, make mud pies in the kitchen sink, and do all manner of iniquity. This did not go over well with our little domestic goddess Sarah. One day she invited a friend to come over and play in the Pretty Pink Princess Kitchen. We told the boys that while the friend was there they were not allowed in the Pretty Pink Princess Kitchen. Those were "fightin' words," and they were not happy about the situation. (Now at ages 18 and 20, they deny their great affinity towards the infamous pink kitchen.) When Sarah and her friend took their dolls out for a stroller ride, one of the boys (name withheld to protect the guilty) went in and took a hammer to the Pretty Pink Princess Kitchen, and soon the Pretty Pink Princess Kitchen was *no more!* This unnamed child had evidently decided that if he could not play with the Pretty Pink Princess Kitchen, then nobody should be able to play with it.

Now, you're probably asking yourself what on earth the destruction of the Pretty Pink Princess Kitchen has to do with your physical body. Well, just as my charming, unnamed son destroyed the Pretty Pink Princess Kitchen in a fit of anger because he was denied access to the kitchen, Satan, too, is throwing the mother of all temper tantrums. He was denied a body and is rather ticked at you for getting one. He is determined to do everything he can to get you to destroy or misuse your body. Be it through breaking the law of chastity, breaking the Word of Wisdom, or somehow desecrating your body—his goal is the same. If he can't play, then he doesn't want you to either. What do you think Satan's weeping, wailing, and gnashing of teeth is all about? This is far more than a big temper tantrum over a Pretty Pink Princess Kitchen. This mortal body was a major step in our eternal progression. In fact, it is one of the few things we get to keep eternally.

So next time you're faced with one of those mother-of-all-temptation moments, just think about who wants you to desecrate or misuse your God-given, sacred body, and remember the parable of the Pretty Pink Princess Kitchen.

The Ski Hill

Years ago on the cover of *Time* magazine was a picture of a boy and a girl around 15 years of age. The heading on the cover read, "Kids, Sex, and Values." Then in the small print below the headline ran the subtitle, "Just do it . . . Just say no . . . What's a kid supposed to think?" The cover depicted the reality that young people today are caught in a battle over shifting values. The struggle they face is to choose between what the world says is acceptable and what the Lord has said is acceptable.

When I taught seminary, for one lesson I would draw a long line from one end of the chalkboard to the other. I would then inform the class that this was the "chastity line." At one end of the line I would write down *holding hands,* and then at the other end *loss of virtue.* I would then, pointing to the beginning of the line, ask what came after holding hands. They would usually list a good-night hug, then maybe a kiss on the cheek, then perhaps a kiss on the lips. After that introduction, I would generally say, "Are there any questions?" At this point, a freshman would typically ask the question the whole class was wondering about: "Brother Jacobs, where is that point on the line?" What was meant by the term *that point on the line?* More bluntly stated, the question he was asking was, "Where is the point on the line that, if I were to cross it, I would have to see my bishop?"

Before I answer this question, I want to you to think about something. Why is it that many youth seem to want to know where "that point on the line" is? You can guess, can't you? They want to know so they can do things right up to that point and then stop, thus avoiding having to see the bishop.

A different question may clarify my point. Are there acts that are sins but that do not require a bishop's involvement? Isn't the reason that one needs to see a bishop the fact that one has done something serious enough in nature that they cannot completely repent without his help? After all, the list of have-to-see-my-bishop sins isn't very long. But there are still plenty of sins *not* on that list. Do you really think that if you have never crossed the "bishop line," no matter how close you have gotten, that you have not sinned? *Wrong!* There is a real danger in thinking you can live very close to that line.

Let me tell you of an experience I had that illustrates the foolishness of this kind of thinking. I am sure most of you have tried your hand at skiing or snowboarding. When I was in high school, I used to go up to Snow Basin and ski. (Skiing is probably an ambitious word to describe what I was doing, but that did not stop me.) On one particular ski trip, I took the lift up to Wildcat, a ski run that was probably beyond my abilities. It was filled with difficult moguls and was very steep—definitely not a beginner's hill.

Anyway, for some strange reason (which had nothing to do with my incredible ski skills) I was not doing very well on this run. I started down the hill, crossed my skis (which, incidently, is not a smart way to ski), and fell down. I got up and looked around to make sure no one was watching. (After all, a guy has got to look cool.) I tried again. Time and time again I would wipe out. My ego was soon smeared all over the face of the mountain. Finally, I stopped partway down the run. I had been on the hill so long that others had made a couple of runs down in the meantime. They would look at me with that "Hey, Slick, weren't you here last time?" look.

As I stood there contemplating my next move, a ski patrolman came up to me. I think he had been watching me for some time, totally entertained I'm sure. He was probably taking footage to show his ski class for a good laugh. He approached me and said, "Looks like you could use some help." *You're quick,* I thought. He pointed down the other side of the ski run and said, "Over there is a trail that leads to Bear Hollow. If I get you there, can you make it down Bear Hollow?" I replied that I could.

He told me that he would point himself toward the trail with his skis wide apart, and all I had to do was simply get behind him, put my skis between his, put my arms around his waist, and off we would go. It sounded a bit humiliating, but at this point humiliation was the least of my worries. He got ready, I put my skis between his, and then I put my arms around his waist. (Perhaps I need to insert here that he was a buff 6'3", 230-pound giant, and I was merely 5'7", 140 pounds.)

Have you ever had something happen that you didn't plan on? I mean, you *really* didn't plan on? Well, as we started across the run, since my skis were close together and I was in a tuck position and he was standing with his skis wide apart, my skis started going faster than his skis. Suddenly, I found myself going underneath him. I held on for dear life. He, of course, couldn't understand what was going on. I found myself sliding down his back, past the seat of his pants, and then my hands started slipping from his waist to his legs. It must have been quite a sight to see. Finally I was underneath him. Then it happened. Because I was pulling on his legs as hard as I could, he finally could not stay up any longer, and he *sat on my face!* Yes, on my face, all 230 pounds of him.

In that position, we rolled down the hill. Once we stopped, he got up and asked, "Are you all right?"

"Sure," I said (not exactly the complete truth, as my goggles had just been smashed permanently into my face).

Now, what does this have to do with the chastity line? Picture the chastity line being like a vertical ski hill. You start down that hill feeling in control, but as the incline steepens, you suddenly find yourself out of control, going faster and faster, headed for destruction. If someone starts down this chastity hill thinking they can stop on a dime, they are truly kidding themselves. President Spencer W. Kimball said:

> He [Satan] knows that if he can get a boy and a girl to sit in a car late enough after a dance, or to park long enough in the dark at the end of the lane, the best boy and the best girl will finally succumb and fall. He knows that all have a limit to their resistance (*Teachings of Spencer W. Kimball,* ed. Edward L. Kimball [1982], 280–281).

I had the wonderful opportunity to be a bishop of a singles ward at Utah State University. You probably won't be surprised to learn that the number-one problem I dealt with, as was the case with every other student-ward bishop, was immorality. Do you think I ever had someone come to confess this sin and say, "The moment I asked her out, I planned on being immoral"? Never! Instead, these youth would come in with their hearts breaking and say, "I can't believe that this happened. I thought I could handle it. I never expected to go this far. It was much harder than I thought."

You see, the farther down the hill you go, the harder it is to stop. Please believe me. The chastity line is much like a steep ski slope and if you're smart, you will keep your "skis," so to speak, at the top of the hill where you can easily control them.

So where on this chastity ski hill is a safe place to be? Let's start at the beginning. Can a young man hold a girl's hand and keep control of his emotions and thoughts? Let's hope so! What about a hug? Listen to President Kimball:

> An embrace may not be immoral, but if the closeness of the body awakens immoral desires, then that is another thing. . . . Two people could embrace, kiss, dance, look, and I can conceive of one of them being immoral and the other innocent of sin (*Teachings of Spencer W. Kimball,* ed. Edward L. Kimball [1982], 282).

How about dancing? Years ago, I went to a high school dance where some of my seminary students were. I went without them knowing, and when word got around that I was there, it was interesting to see how some of my kids reacted. One couple who I knew liked each other tried to stay away from me. I knew they were hiding out somewhere, and I was determined to find them. I decided to go right through the middle of the high school gym and search for them. FYI: This is not a safe place for people to go. "Mine eyes were opened," if you know what I mean. Some of the young people there were holding each other in such a way that I felt I ought to be handing out pass-along cards, the kind that said, "Call your bishop in the morning." I finally found my couple. They did not realize I was there at first, so I just stood there watching them. They were in what could be called the "death clench." Then it happened—they saw me. The young man quickly moved the girl away and released her from the "jaws of hell." "Well, hello, Brother Jacobs," he said rather nervously. I have to wonder and pose the question to you—why did he move her away? Did he know in his heart that maybe, just maybe, he was not keeping the standards of the Church in regards to morality?

The new *For the Strength of Youth* pamphlet provides guidelines about such activities. It says, "Dancing can be fun and can provide an opportunity to meet new people. However, it too can be misused. When dancing, avoid full body contact with your partner. Do not use positions and moves that are suggestive of sexual behavior" (*For the Strength of Youth* [pamphlet, 2001], 21).

I've seen great strength in youth. Once, at an Especially For Youth I spoke at, there was a young man who had asked a young lady to dance. He went to dance with her in a bear-hug style, so the young lady simply moved back a little and then held out her arms in such a way that it informed the young man how she was willing to dance. I was watching this and almost jumped out of my seat to do the Toyota kick and shout "Way to go!" He looked surprised at her reaction, but then, realizing it was this way of dancing or no dance, he took her hands and danced appropriately. What a great example this young woman was. We need more young ladies and young men to take a stand when it comes to dancing.

Remember, the problem with the chastity hill is its steep slope. The farther down the hill, the steeper the incline, and the faster you will go. You must constantly be on your guard against starting down that slippery slope of sin. Once you start down, it's hard to stop. You may even find yourself not wanting to stop. I'm reminded of something I heard many, many years ago. Picture a young lady dating a young man. Both are attracted to each other, and in time, the young man desires a little affection. He kisses her, and she says strongly, "Don't! Stop!" He persists, and again she determinedly says, "Don't! Stop!" However, instead of taking action and running away, she allows him to continue kissing her. This time, her words mean something entirely different. "Don't! Stop!" turns into "Don't stop." Do you understand? Keep your skis safely on top of the chastity hill, and you will stay in control.

Timing is Everything

When you hear the number 16, what comes to mind? Usually one of two words—*dating* or *driving*. If you already have your license, you know that in order to get it, you had to pass a driving test. Don't feel bad if you didn't pass it the first time. I didn't either, and I had a date planned for that night! I finally concluded I'd have to just swing by and pick her up on my two wheels of fury—my bicycle. (This was promising to be a one-time-only date.) Thank goodness I had a friend who already had his license, so we doubled. A week later, on my second attempt, I finally passed. However, my father informed me that before he'd let me drive his car on my own, there were a few rules he wanted to make me aware of. One of the rules was, "Thou shalt not get into a wreck." I figured that if I wanted to keep that rule, I'd be wise to make a few smaller rules. Now I'm the parent and have tried to pass on these same rules to my children. The following story illustrates the usefulness of those "smaller rules."

Once while on a speaking assignment for the Church Educational System, I called home to see how my family was doing. Sarah answered. She was 16 at the time. We chatted for a while, and at the conclusion of our conversation, I told Sarah, "I love you."

She responded, "Do you really?" (That should have given me a clue something was up.)

I said, "Yes, of course."

"Really?" Sarah asked.

"Yes, why do you ask?" I indicated, getting a bit worried.

"Dad, you know the garage?" she said.

"Yes, it was there when I left," I said, wondering where all this was headed.

"Well, you know the garage door?" she continued.

"Yes," I gulped.

She said, "Well, you know how when you back out of the garage, there is the little button?"

"You mean the one that opens the garage door?" I answered.

"Yes, that one," she replied. Well, by now I had a suspicion something was up.

"What happened?" I said as calmly as I could. Sarah finally told me.

"Well, I was backing out of the garage, and I forgot to push the button, so I ran into the garage door with the car."

"Really?" I asked in amazement. I have to admit that it was rather hard for me to understand how she could not notice the garage door was not opened when she was backing out, but then, I am not a *teenager!*

Now, no one would argue that if you want to keep the rule, "Thou shalt not get into a wreck," it's probably smart to also have rules such as, "Thou shalt pay attention while driving," or "Thou shalt turn your brain on while driving." It is the same when it comes to dating. If you want to keep the big rules, keep the little ones. Those smaller rules help you keep the big ones. The dating age set by the Church is one of those small rules—seemingly insignificant to some—that help you keep the big rule, the law of chastity. It is the same with the Church's stand on avoiding steady dating when you are young. I am amazed at how so many young people want to throw these smaller rules out, thinking they are unimportant.

For the Strength of Youth clearly gives some very good reasons to heed these smaller rules. It says, "Do not date until you are *at least* 16 years old. Dating before then can lead to immorality, limit the number of other young people you meet, and deprive you of experiences that will help you choose an eternal partner" (*For the Strength of Youth* [pamphlet, 2001], 24; emphasis added). Notice it doesn't say "about 16." It says not to date until you are "at least 16." Not "just about" or "close to," or "almost 16." It goes on to say, "The Lord has made us attractive one to another for a great purpose. But this very attraction becomes as a powder keg unless it is kept under control. . . . It is for this reason that the Church counsels against early dating" (24). President Kimball also spoke on the importance of waiting for this age.

> Any dating or pairing off in social contacts should be postponed until *at least* the age of 16 or older, and even then there should still be much judgment used in selections and in the seriousness. Young people should still limit the close contacts for several years, since the boy will be going on his mission when he is 19 years old.
>
> Dating and especially steady dating in the early teens is most hazardous. It distorts the whole picture of life ("President Kimball Speaks Out on Morality," *Ensign*, Nov. 1980, 96; emphasis added).

I know of one young lady who badly wanted to go to her high school's homecoming dance, but the dance was a couple of weeks before she turned 16. She made up her mind that if she was asked, she wouldn't go. A couple of weeks after the dance, she turned 16, and she said to me, "I did it! I waited. It feels so good to know I waited. There will be other dances and other chances to date." She said it felt great to know that she had followed the counsel of the prophet. She would forever be able to look her children in the eye and tell them that they, too, could wait.

I was teaching seminary one day when a student came up to me and asked if she could talk for a second. We went into my office, and I could tell she was nervous. After some chitchat, she opened up and said, "I've done some really bad things, and I'm afraid."

She told me she had lived in California earlier in her life. When she was only 13 or 14, an older guy who, unfortunately, was looking for a younger girl to prey on, had asked her out on a date. She knew the guideline of the Church was to wait until she was at least 16, but he was cute and she was flattered that an older guy was interested in her, so she began to date him. Her family was not very active in the Church, and they didn't object. She dated this young man for a while, too young to really understand his predatory nature, but he knew what he was doing. She ended up pregnant and alone. He wasn't interested in her anymore. She decided to place the child up for adoption, but she felt horrible. She went through the pain of giving up her beautiful child, realizing it was best for both of them, but it was nonetheless a painful choice. Her self-esteem had been destroyed, and she wondered who would want her now.

She ended up dating other young men who weren't good for her, and she eventually ended up pregnant again. Distraught, she didn't dare tell her mother, so at the tender age of 16 and all alone, she found a clinic and had an abortion. When she came to me, she indicated she had talked with her bishop about everything else but couldn't bring herself to tell him about the abortion. She felt guilty and ashamed.

I was able to make contact with her bishop, and he helped her through the long process of true repentance. But what a price to pay! I have wondered many times how different her life would have been had she just kept the seemingly simple "wait until you're 16" rule. Over and over, she told me how she wished she would have waited to date until she was more mature and had been able to see more clearly. The "fun" of early dating had caused nothing but heartache.

In the *New Era* one month, a young lady wrote:

> When I was 14, I decided that pairing up with one "special" boyfriend wasn't "dating," so it was okay. It began as a way to be more popular, but soon I was lying to my parents so I could spend time alone with him. Over the ten months we were together, my testimony was slowly weakened, and eventually I had problems with the law of chastity. Since then I've talked with my bishop and repented, but it was a long, difficult, and painful process. I hurt myself, my parents, and the Lord. It opened the door to many other temptations bit by bit and made the important things in life seem foolish, and the wrong things appear right. My parents and bishop showed me nothing but love as they tried to help me return to the

Lord's favor. How much I wish I'd had the strength when I was 14 to stand alone and be different! ("Q&A: Questions and Answers" *New Era*, July 1995, 17–18).

It really is such a simple thing to wait to date. I can promise you that the earth will still continue to rotate and the sun will still come up in the East and set in the West if you do. Most important, you will have the peace of mind that you kept this simple rule given by the prophet. Remember the scripture that says, "By small and simple things are great things brought to pass" (Alma 37:6). The Lord's simple rules lead to great joy in our lives. Never minimize the simple rules that the prophets have given us. They are given to keep us safe and bring us joy.

Another guideline is the *type* of dating you should be doing when you begin dating. It is so sad to see young people quickly get into the single-dating scene. They miss the fun of group dating, and often end up excluding friends and even family. They can become so focused on their single relationship that they miss getting to know others, which is exactly the purpose for the early years of group dating. Notice what was suggested in the *New Era:*

> Of course, dating is meant to be a way of getting to know members of the opposite sex as you prepare for marriage. However, at 16, you should be thinking more about going out in groups or on double dates. It's lots of fun. Group dating is great for making friends, and it involves a lot less pressure. And in group dates, the burden of paying for the activity doesn't always fall completely on the young men ("Q&A: Questions and Answers," *New Era*, Aug. 1998, 17).

President Hinckley reinforced this guideline when he said:

> When you are young, do not get involved in steady dating. When you reach an age where you think of

marriage, then is the time to become so involved. But
you boys who are in high school don't need this, and
neither do the girls. . . . Have a wonderful time with
the young women. Do things together, but do not get
too serious too soon. You have missions ahead of you,
and you cannot afford to compromise this great
opportunity and responsibility ("Some Thoughts on
Temples, Retention of Converts, and Missionary
Service," *Ensign*, Nov. 1997, 49).

Are you willing to simply believe and obey the prophet?

I realize that when the young men return from their missions, it's
appropriate to be looking for a companion, and that is the point
when dating exclusively becomes necessary. Before then, group dating
is a safer path. Rarely have young people had major problems with
chastity while in the presence of other young people. One fine young
man told me that he and two of his friends decided they would help
each other stay away from temptation. If ever there was a time that
any of them felt temptation, they would simply say, "Piccadilly" and
the others would realize it was a distress signal and come help their
friend out. Sounds crazy, but it worked.

The average beginning age for dating in the United States is
around 13 years of age. Studies show that the earlier people date, the
greater chance they have of being immoral.

For his doctoral dissertation, a friend of mine, Bruce Monson,
examined factors that help young people stay morally clean. He used
data supplied by LDS and non-LDS juniors in two different high
schools. One of the most crucial factors in staying morally clean for
these young people was choosing to wait until age 16 to date. His
findings were published, in part, in the *New Era*. He found, "While
about 70 percent of those who waited until 16 had avoided immoral
behavior, more than 80 percent of those who dated before age 16 had
become sexually involved enough to required a bishop's help for
repentance" ("Speaking of Kissing," *New Era*, June 2001, 36).

So much for those who think it's not going to make any difference
if they date earlier! I hope all the youth (as well as adults) who read
this will see the wisdom of waiting to begin dating. Monson's studies

also dealt with steady dating. In the survey, 95 couples were dating steadily. Of those, 6 had never made out, 18 had stopped at making out, while 17 had stopped at petting, and 54 had gone all the way!

A couple of years ago a man from BYU spoke to the faculty at the Logan Institute of Religion. He discussed research done to show if there was any evidence that LDS youth are different from their counterparts in the United States. He talked about "delinquent activity" such as smoking, drinking, using pot, and sexual intimacy. His findings were rather interesting. LDS high school seniors were less likely to be involved in each of the behaviors just mentioned. When it came to having sex by the time they were seniors, 10 percent of LDS boys and 17 percent of LDS girls had lost their virtue. (In the same study, 77 percent of non-LDS boys and 66 percent of non-LDS girls had engaged in sex.) While it's sad that *any* Latter-day Saint young people have had sex outside marriage, the numbers do show that we, as a whole, are different.

How grateful we should be for living prophets to guide us in the path that will protect us from making major mistakes! The counsel to wait to date until 16, and then to group date, is given to protect us and keep us safe.

Crossing the Line

While teaching seminary, I had a young man come into my office and ask the following question: "How do I know if I have to see my bishop?" This was one of my best young men, as well as someone the girls would have called a "hottie." He was strong, handsome (not that I rate guys personally, but the girls told me he was), and a spiritually strong kid.

"What happened?" I asked.

"Well," he began, "I was with this girl on a date and we kissed a few times. Then," he continued, "she started to put the moves on me."

I was a little taken aback. "Say that again? *She* puts the moves on you?" I asked.

"Yes, honest, she did," he replied.

"What did you do?" I had to ask.

"I quickly stopped her and told her I don't do those kind of things." He then told me he immediately drove her home and then went straight to his home, repenting all the way. He asked, "Do I have to see my bishop?"

Now, my young friends, does he? Where is "the line" that, if crossed, you must see your bishop to help you in the repentance process? The young man asked if I would talk to his bishop, and I did so. I told him what the young man had said, and when I got to the "she put the moves on him" part, the bishop said, "Did you say *she?*" I told him yes.

"What did he do?" the bishop inquired. I told him that the young man stopped her and took her right home. The bishop then said, "Give him a MEDAL!" We talked a little while longer and hung up. I told the young man what his bishop had said and advised him to be careful about the young women he picked to ask out. He promised he would. A couple of years later, after he served a wonderful mission, he married a beautiful young lady in the temple. The point of the story? Don't think that if you're a guy, you're always the one to decide whether or not temptation arises. Girls need to be told where your standards are as well. It's becoming more and more common that temptation is invited by *both* genders!

In a talk I gave to my ward when I was a bishop, I felt impressed to use Elder Richard G. Scott's talk from a general conference. It is a fairly unique talk because he answers several questions from youth he's met across the world. It is helpful for youth who have questions about "the line."

> Question: They always tell us we shouldn't become sexually involved, but they never tell us the limits. What are they?
>
> Answer: Any sexual intimacy outside the bonds of marriage—I mean any intentional contact with the sacred, private parts of another's body, with or without clothing—is a sin and is forbidden by God. It is also a transgression to intentionally stimulate these emotions within your own body.

Later in the same talk, this question was asked:

> Question: How do you go about repenting after a sexual sin is committed? What sins should you tell the bishop?
>
> Answer: All of the sexual transgressions we have discussed require sincere repentance with the participation of the bishop. Should you have done any of this, repent now ("Making the Right Choices," *Ensign,* Nov. 1994, 38).

In another talk, Elder Scott made this statement:

Strongly tied to the sacred, private parts of the body are powerful emotions intended to be used within the covenant of marriage between a man and woman in ways that are appropriate and acceptable to them both. . . . These emotions are not to be stimulated or used for personal gratification outside of the covenant of marriage. Do not touch the private, sacred parts of another person's body to stimulate those emotions. Do not allow anyone to do that with you, with or without clothing. Do not arouse those emotions in your own body. These things are wrong. Do not do them. Such practices would undermine your ability to be inspired by the Holy Ghost in the vitally important decisions you must make for your future ("The Power of Righteousness," *Ensign,* Nov. 1998, 68).

After I read the earlier statement by Elder Scott to the youth in my student ward, I found several young people who desired to see me. As we talked, they indicated that because of what they'd learned from those statements, they realized that they had crossed the line. Some said that they had tried earlier to excuse their behavior, but with such straightforward counsel, they could no longer hide under the illusion that they didn't need to talk with me about their problems. How grateful I was for the directness of Elder Scott and others.

If any of you reading this discover that you have crossed that line, I plead with you to do the right thing. Contact your bishop and talk with him. Clear up your past. Get straight with the Lord, and in time you'll feel better about yourself and your relationship with God. It may not be easy, but I know from my own experience as a bishop the great blessing confession and repentance can bring. I could see it in the eyes of each truly repentant person.

To Kiss or Not to Kiss

Some years ago there was a young man who had just returned from a two-year mission. After being home for a month or two, he started school and decided that it was time for him to start actually noticing girls (since he hadn't done that in two years). He approached his mom one day and announced that he'd found a girl in one of his classes that he wanted to go out with. She encouraged him in this and told him that it wouldn't be out of order if, at the end of a date with the young woman, he presented her with a small thank-you gift. He contemplated what he could give as a gift, finally deciding that candy would be just the thing. So, he went into a candy store one day and browsed through the impressive selection. Finally, he approached the manager and asked the man for a one-pound, a two-pound, and a three-pound box of chocolates. The manager filled his order and the young man paid for it. As the young man was preparing to leave, the manager stopped him and asked, "I just have to know—how come you're getting *that much* chocolate? I mean, six pounds of chocolate is quite a bit."

The young man looked around to make sure no one else was in the store before he replied, "Because I have a date tonight."

Somewhat confused, the manager asked, "What does that have to do with all these chocolates?"

"Well," the young man continued, "my mom told me that at the end of a date I should present the girl with a gift, and I decided that how the girl treats me on the date will determine how much chocolate she gets. You see," he went on, "if the girl I take out tonight sits on her side of the car *the whole time* and doesn't even let me put my arm around her or get close to her or anything, I guess I'll give her the one-pound box of chocolates.

"But, if she warms up a little, maybe allows me to cuddle up with her just a bit and even put my arm around her, and if I get even just one good, solid kiss, well, she gets the two-pound box of chocolates."

The manager looked somewhat skeptical, but he allowed the young man to continue.

"And if we can have just a good, solid make-out session, she's gonna get the *three-pound box* of chocolates, no question about it."

The manager didn't say much, just shook his head disapprovingly as the young man left. The young man covered the boxes of chocolates in the back of his car, then went home to prepare for his date.

That evening, he approached the house of his date and knocked on the door. When he was invited inside, he realized this girl came from the classic Mormon family. He also learned that their rule was that he had to meet the entire family, which meant that all 14 kids lined up in the front room (except for his date) and inspected him while he waited for the girl to come out. She eventually did, and as soon as her parents walked into the room, the young man immediately said, "You know, I think we should have a prayer before we leave." Then he dropped to his knees and began praying. Though somewhat confused, everyone immediately followed suit, including the parents. The young man prayed for 20 minutes—covering every subject and praying for nearly everything he could think of. After a while, as he sensed that the children were growing restless, he ended the prayer, he and his date said good-bye to everyone and then left.

They got in his car and rode in shocked silence for several minutes before the girl finally spoke. "I have to tell you, I had no idea you were so religious," she said.

"Well," the young man said in a weak voice, "I had no idea your dad managed a candy store."

I love telling that story just for the sheer fun of the reactions I get from people. When adults hear the phrase *make out*, they freeze, but when they get to the end of the story, they love it. Why do they react that way? What if the same situation occurred with the exception that the young man never met the parents, but his date returned home that evening carrying three pounds of chocolates? Would you be ashamed of the young man? Would you feel bad and embarrassed for the young woman? Probably. Does our reaction to the story say something about what we know to be right when it comes to physical affection and treating others with respect, particularly when it involves something as intimate as kissing?

Do you remember the movie *The Little Mermaid?* It's a Disney classic. One of my favorite scenes is when Ariel and Eric are in the boat. It's a beautiful evening; the moon is shining bright. Eric, of course, hasn't heard a lot from Ariel, seeing that the Octopus Woman has her voice, so he's trying to make conversation. Well, Scuttle tries to sing, and it's a disaster. Along comes good ol' Sebastian with the philosophy that "if you want something done, you've got to do it yourself." The music starts, and he begins singing, "There you see her, sitting there across the way. She don't got a lot to say, but there's something about her. And you don't why, but you're dying to try, you want to kiss the girl." The song continues with more and more animals pitching in to help.

Eric and Ariel start moving closer together. Do you remember the first time you saw it? What were you thinking during this scene? If you're a red-blooded male, you were probably thinking, "All right! They're finally going to kiss!" As you were waiting for them to lock lips, suddenly the boat tipped over. Were you ticked? Shoot the eels, I say!

At the end of the movie, Eric and Ariel are married, and her father, Triton, comes out of the water and they finally kiss. What kind of kiss was it? I call it the "Disney kiss." Tender and sweet. But isn't there more than one way to kiss?

I remember once having a beautiful young lady come talk to me as her bishop. She had always been active in the Church. She read her scriptures, prayed, and kept the commandments. When she came in, I could tell she was noticeably upset, nervous, and embarrassed. She then told me her problem. She had been dating a young man for some time. He had received his mission call and was going to enter the MTC soon. They had been very careful and had kept the standards of the Church beautifully. Then, the night before he was going to be set apart, they were together, and they kissed. It was a different kiss, with more emotion and passion than ever before. She told me they both immediately stopped, looked at each other, and realized they'd better quit kissing. I'll never forget how guilty she felt as I talked with her. She said this kiss had aroused feelings she never knew she had. When they let their guard down, those feelings suddenly surfaced, and both she and the young man were surprised and troubled by what had taken place. Take warning: It is deceptively easy for a simple "Disney kiss" to turn into something much, much more. You need to keep your guard *constantly* up. The feelings that come when you aren't being careful should be saved for marriage.

On television, in the movies, and in the media as a whole, what kind of kissing is promoted? The Disney kiss? Hardly! It's the let-her-up-for-air, she-can't-breathe kiss. All kisses are not the same. Would you be willing to admit that there are certain types of kisses that might be okay while dating and yet others that are not appropriate for anything outside of a marriage relationship?

When I was in high school, I went to a youth stake dance. You know, the ones where the guys hang out either by the refreshments or in the halls while the girls talk about how immature the guys are. Anyway, in my "maturity," I'd actually been talking with a young lady of whom I was very fond, and finally we decided to go outside and do some more "talking." After chatting for a while, I decided it was "time." Well, I went in for the kill. As I approached, her eyes closed. (Mine remained open because I wanted to make sure I hit the target and not her nose.) Just as I was ready to kiss her, she opened her mouth wide. I honestly had not seen a kiss like that—*ever*. At that time, the only kisses I had seen on television were short and sweet. I stopped short of my "target" and just looked at her open mouth, staring at those big, ugly tonsils. I remember thinking that if I went any closer, I could get my face sucked in there and never come out alive! A few seconds went by, though I'm sure it seemed like an eternity, before she looked up and said, "What are you doing?" I replied, "What are *you* doing?" She looked somewhat embarrassed and answered, "I thought we were going to *kiss*." I answered, "So did I, but you have to close your mouth first." Well, needless to say, no kissing went on that night. I left wondering what in the world she was doing. She probably left wondering what part of the world I was from.

I think you know what kind of kiss I had a near miss with that night. Is it still called a "French kiss"? Where does that kiss belong on the chastity hill? Would you acknowledge that the French kiss is a little more intense than the Disney kiss? President Kimball had the following to say about such kisses:

> Kissing has been prostituted and has degenerated to develop and express lust instead of affection, honor, and admiration. To kiss in casual dating is asking for trouble. . . . What is miscalled the "soul kiss" [French kiss to us] is an abomination and stirs passion to the eventual loss of virtue. Even if timely courtship justifies the kiss it should be a clean, decent, sexless one. . . . If the "soul kiss" with its passion were eliminated from dating there would be an immediate upswing in chastity and honor (*Teachings of Spencer W. Kimball,* ed. Edward L. Kimball [1982], 281).

Isaiah 57:3–4 also talks about inappropriate types of kisses. "But draw near hither, ye sons of the sorceress, the seed of the adulterer and the whore. Against whom do ye sport yourselves? against whom make ye a wide mouth, and draw out the tongue? are ye not children of transgression . . . ?" Now I may be old, but that sounds like a current definition of French-kissing to me.

Often youth do not understand why kissing can be dangerous. Remember the ski hill? How far down can you go and still stay in control? A French kiss is dangerous because of the feelings it stirs up, feelings that can overwhelm an otherwise good young person. Notice how parents and young people were counseled back in 1984 by President Kimball. I know, you probably weren't even born yet, but listen anyway. It still applies today:

> Unless forearmed, it is difficult for youth to distinguish where indiscretions will lead. The first "movie" kiss becomes "making out," and the "making out" becomes fornication before they fully realize the power of sexual feelings. These forces are powerful; they were *meant* to be. But they were meant for mature couples in the sanctity of marriage.

We must clearly explain to our children that passionate kissing and "making out" should be left until *after* marriage. Too many young couples falsely believe that because they are dating or engaged they can relax these constraints. Yet it is during this emotion-filled time that the greatest care should be taken to build and preserve a virtuous relationship ("Talking with Your Children about Moral Purity," *Ensign,* Dec. 1986, 60).

Did you catch one important phrase? "These forces [meaning sexual feelings] are powerful; they were *meant* to be. But they were meant for mature couples in the sanctity of marriage."

When I served my mission in Alaska, the missionary discussions were different. They were pretty much written out for us. There was a discussion on keeping the commandments, and one concept in that discussion dealt with the law of chastity. I was amazed at how differently some people in the world viewed this important principle. One of the lines from the discussion said, "The feelings behind this are powerful, powerful enough to persuade men to take on the responsibilities of a family. But because they are strong, they can be misused."

When you start down the chastity hill, there are emotions and feelings that are very powerful. The problem is that if you let these emotions out early, it's hard to stop. French-kissing and making out can evoke these emotions before you marry. So, if you really want to keep your skis on the top of the hill where you are still in control, make a hard-and-fast rule that in your dating years, there will be no French-kissing and definitely no making out.

Elder Richard G. Scott exposes some of the lies Satan uses to get us to rationalize immoral behavior. "Satan tempts one to believe that there are allowable levels of physical contact between consenting individuals who seek the powerful stimulation of emotions they produce, and if kept within bounds, no harm will result. As a witness of Jesus Christ, I testify that is absolutely false" ("Making the Right Choices," *Ensign,* Nov. 1994, 38).

There is another very important reason to be ever so careful. This reason is found in Doctrine and Covenants 42:23: "And he that looketh upon a woman to lust after her shall deny the faith, *and shall not have the Spirit*" (emphasis added).

The Spirit is something you cannot afford to lose! Most of you are moving towards or are already of an age where you will face some of the most important decisions you will ever have to make in your life—where to go to school, whom to marry, what profession you will choose, etc. I'm willing to guess you're not simply going to flip a coin to decide these big decisions. You'll pray like you've never prayed before for guidance and direction. Aren't you going to want the help of the Holy Ghost in making those decisions? If so, you must live worthy to receive His inspiration.

Elder Richard G. Scott has also spoken about the ramification of not living in accordance with God's law but still asking for His guidance.

> Not all our prayers will be answered as we wish. It is not always easy to know the will of the Lord, yet there are some things we can be certain of. He will never ask us to do anything that is not completely in harmony with His teachings. We cannot count on help if we are immoral or otherwise deliberately disobedient unless we sincerely repent. One who prays to know if another is to be the eternal companion while violating in any degree the law of chastity has little hope of receiving confirmation without repentance ("Obtaining Help from the Lord," *Ensign*, Nov. 1991, 84).

The very thing we need to help us make decisions and warn us against temptation is lost if we violate this important principle of chastity. It's simply not worth it when compared with the guilty feelings and loss of the Spirit.

Young ladies, if a young man ever tries to kiss you inappropriately, stop him then and there, even if he is as cute as can be. Never lower your standards! Letting him know where you stand will either increase his respect for you or cause him to leave you alone. If he leaves you for another willing to give in, he wasn't worth keeping in the first place. If he realizes your standard and respects it, so much the better for both of you.

I have a beautiful daughter named Sarah. Her name means "Princess." When she came into the world, I looked at my beautiful little girl and was overwhelmed by the knowledge that Heavenly Father had entrusted her to me. When I had the privilege to give her a name and a blessing, I mentioned at least three times chastity and virtue. Sarah and I have talked openly about this subject over the years many, many times.

One young man who didn't know her strong standards asked her out. He had met her at a fireside I had given in his stake where Sarah had sung. At the end of the date, he mistakenly asked, "Don't I at least get a kiss?" Boy was he dumb!

"NO," Sarah said. Needless to say, that was their last date. While he was amazed at her conviction, she was amazed at his stupidity. She had made a decision early on that, contrary to popular belief, she was *not* going to kiss a lot of frogs along the way before she found her prince. In fact, the only young man she ever kissed (other than in a musical) was her future husband, and it was his first kiss at 24! Remember, you can croak with the frogs on the lily pad, but you don't have to kiss them!

I remember kissing my wife for the first time. We had been getting to know one another for quite some time, and I was taking her home at the end of a date. She was so beautiful, and I was so impressed by her goodness. As I looked at her and realized that she was going out with me, I thought, "You lucky dog, you!" I leaned over and kissed her—not on the lips, but instead on her forehead. A clean, decent, sexless kiss. Nearly two years later (it took her a long time to decide if the Lord wanted her to take me on as an eternal service project), we knelt at an altar in the Salt Lake Temple. As we were sealed, the temple president, who had performed the ceremony, said, "You may now kiss your bride." I leaned across the altar and kissed her forehead, just as I had in the beginning. The sealer, as well as several others, I'm sure, were a little shocked. The sealer then said, "Young man, you can do better than that." I did!

Heed the Warning Signs

While serving as bishop of a student ward, I had somewhere in the neighborhood of 26 or so engaged couples at one time. That made for a rather busy schedule in the bishop's office since I made a rule that each couple had to touch base with me each week just to make sure everything was okay as their engagement went along. It was hard at times for these couples—after all, once you've made your choice of whom to marry, the feelings of love that brought you together can become even stronger. But it was also wonderful to see their desires to remain clean and worthy of the temple.

I would usually find out a certain couple was engaged by the way they approached me. The female was always the dead giveaway. She would come running towards me with her hand extended out, fingers down, so I could see the flash of the diamond. She was so excited and thrilled, and I'd set up an appointment so I could talk with the couple. They first had to tell me all about getting engaged, which inevitably led to hearing every little detail about how he popped the question. Finally, we would talk about the temple and being worthy to enter it, which included a discussion of the rules they should live by to be worthy to enter the temple. The how-to-stay-morally-clean-rules for an engaged couple aren't all that different than the rules for dating, so what specifically are the some of the rules outlined by the Brethren?

Elder Hartman Rector Jr., who was a navy pilot for some 26 years, gives a great analogy. He said:

> In my experience, I have found that it is very, very dangerous to fly just high enough to miss the treetops. I

spent twenty-six years flying the navy's airplanes. It was very exciting to see how close I could fly to the trees. This is called "flat hatting" in the navy, and it is extremely dangerous. When you are flying just high enough to miss the trees and your engine coughs once, you are in the trees.

Now let's pretend that the navy had a commandment—"Thou shalt not fly thy airplane in the trees." As a matter of fact, they did have such a commandment. In order to really be free of the commandment, it becomes necessary for me to add a commandment of my own to the navy's commandment, such as, "Thou shalt not fly thy airplane closer than 5,000 feet to the trees." When you do this, you make the navy's commandment of not flying in the trees easy to live, and the safety factor is tremendously increased ("Live above the Law to Be Free," *Ensign*, Jan. 1973, 131).

So when I'd talk to the engaged couples in my ward, I would outline the rules that would keep them flying "5,000 feet" above any trouble. There is nothing more tragic than when a couple heading toward a temple marriage finds themselves "crashing into the trees" and losing, for a time, their opportunity to be sealed in the temple.

In one of my institute classes, I taught a wonderful couple who were engaged but had a difficult time with the "5,000 foot" rule. They were very at ease showing physical affection during class, which was a bit distracting at times. I clearly remember the night before their wedding when I received a call from the young lady. I had been invited to their temple wedding the next day. With all the courage she could muster, she explained that the wedding would not be in the temple as planned, but rather at her stake center. I could sense her great pain as she told me this, and I wanted to comfort her and tell her it would be all right. This was not the wedding this young couple had dreamed of, and I couldn't help but wonder if simple obedience to a precautionary rule would have prevented their heartbreak.

Years ago, a wedding invitation arrived at my in-laws' home while we were visiting. When they opened it up, there was a couple's wedding announcement with a picture of the Logan Temple in the background. But a big, black X was marked through the temple, and also blacked out were the words *sealed in the Logan LDS temple for time and all eternity.*

Young people, there is nothing more heartrending than to see wonderful, wonderful couples whose temple marriage plans are thwarted when they, in a moment of carelessness, fly too close to the trees. Remember to listen to the guidelines of our leaders, who counsel us to stay as far away from temptation as we can.

Notice what Elder M. Russell Ballard has said:

> Our youth seem confused about the definition of moral cleanliness. Some young men and women take a certain definition and then push it to the limits to see how far they can go without being immoral by that definition. I suggest an opposite approach. . . . Some standards must not be compromised. . . . You can know the correct standards of moral conduct by following the promptings of the Spirit. These promptings never will lead you to do anything that makes you feel uncomfortable, unclean, or ashamed. . . .
>
> Once you understand the standards, you must determine that you will live by them. . . .You must be as Joseph who fled from the presence of Potiphar's wife rather than sin against God. (See Gen. 39:7–12.) You must avoid moral misconduct by making a firm decision to avoid compromising situations and to stand firm for what is right. You must have self-control and high goals. I urge every one of you tonight to set a goal to be morally clean, if you have not already done so ("Purity Precedes Power," *Ensign,* Nov. 1990, 37).

Are you willing to take Elder Ballard's challenge?

Most of you have probably already had the wonderful experience of taking driver's education. You were likely taught how to handle dangerous situations on the highways, to slow down if it was wet or if conditions on the road were dangerous. You were taught what each warning sign on the road meant and how you should act in accordance. Finally, they probably showed you the gruesome movies about what happens when you do not drive defensively and safely. When you knew all the textbook answers, they put you out on the road to see how well you listened during those long, boring hours in class. How foolish you would be to ignore the rules and warning signs. Likewise, the Lord has given you warning signs in dating. Those warnings are there to protect you from getting in spiritually dangerous territory. Make up your mind now to heed the signs the Lord has given to keep you safe.

Playing by the Rules

What comes to your mind when you think of church basketball? You've probably heard the statement, "Church basketball is the only brawl that begins and ends with prayer." When I was a new seminary teacher, I was on our church basketball team. With my incredible 5'7" frame, I was certainly a major force to be reckoned with. At one particular game, several of the parents of my students were there watching. Unfortunately, a couple of the guys on my team were determined to win at all costs. They simply didn't care to play fair. At this particular game, within the first quarter we had been given two technical fouls by two teammates' rather blatant disregard for the rules. A third would result in the game being stopped and our team being given a loss. I remember being embarrassed by these teammates, especially after the final play of the game went something like this: One of these guys had the ball, and he was headed across midcourt at full speed. An opposing player placed himself in front of him, solid and in position, but that didn't stop my teammate. He literally ran over the other player. The call was obvious to all present except our rather arrogant jock, and he was called with "charging." The poor player on the other team could hardly get up! The referee started down to the other end of the court, and what did my brilliant teammate do? He took the ball and, with all his might, threw it directly at the head of the referee. It flew past his ear and slammed into the wall at the other end of the court. A third technical was called, and the game was over—all because of someone's inability to realize that he wasn't above the rules of the game.

Just as there are rules in basketball, the "dating game" has rules too. Just like the guy on our team hurt all of us by breaking the rules of the game, breaking the dating rules can hurt far more individuals than the ones directly involved. Think of the many unwanted pregnancies; unwed mothers; and parents, friends, or relatives affected by a loved one breaking the law of chastity.

Elder Hartman Rector Jr. listed several rules that will help young people stay away from temptation ("Live above the Law to Be Free," *Ensign*, Jan. 1973, 131). Here are four points from his list.

> 1. Never go into a house alone with a member of the opposite sex.

This may seem like a ridiculous little rule to you, and yet as a bishop I saw its importance time and time again. An empty house is too private. There is no one around to help keep displays of affection from going too far. There are obviously times when young people may want to be alone, but try to "be alone" in a more public place, like outside or on a walk. Don't put yourself in a position that may cause great temptation.

> 2. Never, ever, ever enter a bedroom alone with a member of the opposite sex.

Do I have to explain this one? It's a no-brainer. I can remember living in a house with 11 other guys. That's right—12 guys in one house, 6 upstairs and 6 downstairs. Most of the guys were returned missionaries, but when I lived with them I had not gone on a mission yet. There was a young lady I was dating at that time, and I brought her over to the house one day. Well, you can probably imagine the noise and craziness with everyone living there. There was no place for just the two of us to talk, so without really thinking, I took her into my little (and I mean little) bedroom. We'd only been in there a couple of minutes when someone knocked on the door. I went over and opened it, and there stood several of my roommates. They were all smiles, big and bright. Then they began singing a Primary tune: "I have two little hands folded snugly and tight. They are tiny and weak, but they know what is right!" I got the hint and looked at the young lady, who started to laugh. I realized how foolish it was, even under the most innocent of circumstances, to be in a bedroom alone with a member of the opposite sex. Boy was I grateful for good roommates.

Several times as a bishop, I had couples who had not obeyed this guideline come to my office. They thought they could put themselves in a dangerous situation, stay in control, and fly just barely above the trees. But when they were in compromising situations, emotion overcame reason, and they fell. Each couple would explain that they had just innocently wanted moments alone, but the outcome was tragic.

3. Do not neck (i.e., make out) or pet.

You do not have to be a rocket scientist to know the importance of this rule. I realize that the scriptures don't actually say, "Thou shalt not *neck* or *pet*," but President Kimball said:

> Among the most common sexual sins our young people commit are necking and petting. Not only do these improper relations often lead to fornication, pregnancy, and abortions—all ugly sins—but in and of themselves they are pernicious evils, and it is often difficult for youth to distinguish where one ends and another begins. . . . And the Lord perhaps was referring to this even when in our own time he was reiterating the Ten Commandments, "Neither commit adultery, nor kill, *nor do anything like unto it*" (*The Miracle of Forgiveness*, [1969], 65–66; emphasis added).

Do you remember why certain behavior before marriage must be avoided? The feelings that are created can be powerful! The more comfortable you become in that dangerous territory, the easier it gets to move into forbidden territory. And forbidden territory is where grievous sin takes place. *It's not worth it!*

4. Never park on a lonely road with just the two of you alone.

One time during high school, I was on a triple date with two of my friends. I had been lined up with their dates' best friend, who lived in the foothills of another city. After we dropped her off at the end of the evening, we went up the road to turn around and found ourselves at a lookout of sorts. We were surprised by what we saw. There, overlooking the city, were several well-spaced cars. After we watched for some time, it wasn't hard to determine that the couple in each car was *not* looking at the city lights. We all decided to do something to help these poor couples see the error of their ways, so I slowly drove up to one car with my headlights off. When I was very close to their car, I suddenly turned my lights on high beam! You should have seen the couple move. We got quite a laugh as we drove quickly away, our suspicions about what they were doing confirmed. It is simply dangerous territory to be alone in a car in a deserted area.

Each year at Utah State University, the bishops try to make up a list of other "don'ts" for dating. Several of these are helpful for keeping youth on track while dating and are worth adding to our list.

5. No back rubs.

I realize that a good back rub can be extremely relaxing. However, I also know how dangerous they can be. Becoming too familiar with each others' bodies brings a sense of liberties you are not entitled to while single! If something is wrong with your back, see a chiropractor!

6. Do not lie down by each other.

Such activity is playing with fire. When you watch television or listen to the stereo, sit up! When you give each other a good-night kiss, stand up! Then go HOME . . . ALONE!

7. No late hours.

What good can really be accomplished after midnight? Once again, as a bishop I would find that greater problems arose with my youth when they were together late at night. Many would find themselves getting tired but not wanting to go home yet. Please remember that when you are tired, your brain *is not* completely functioning. (It's worse than normal teenage brain dysfunction.) When you are tired, please realize your resistance is lower and it can become harder to run from temptation. Whether or not you feel the date is "over," if you are tired, go home!

8. Decide in advance your rules for dating.

I cannot emphasize this rule enough—it is so critical. Decide while you are young exactly what your rules and standards will be, and then do not let anyone change those standards. You need to make the decisions well in advance of the heat of the moment. If a date refuses to follow your rules and seems to always be pushing the limit, drop him or her immediately. Do not allow your standards to be lowered at any time. Set the barriers and rules before and not during temptation.

9. Discuss your dating rules with those you date.

This rule applies more to those after a mission and in college who are in a more serious relationship, but it is certainly useful for any type of dating situation. I found that those couples in serious relationships who talked openly about their rules in dating were usually better at keeping those rules. Discuss them while your minds are clear and uncluttered by emotion of the moment. Then stick to them!

10. Do not think you are the exception to the rules!

After I taught one of my institute classes about the dating rules, one young lady came up and expressed how ridiculous and unnecessary she thought some of them were. She frankly told me that she didn't think the Brethren would ever have these stupid rules. I remember thinking how foolish this young lady was. Instead of flying 5,000 feet above the trees, she wanted to see what it was like just a few feet above them—and risk having something happen that would put her in forbidden territory. I plead with you to realize that rules are not given as a punishment—as something designed and imposed on you to destroy your weekend or your fun—but rather to keep you safe and free from danger.

I'm sure we could probably list many, many more dating rules and cautions, but the bottom line is this: Use wisdom, the counsel of the prophets, the *For the Strength of Youth* pamphlet, your leaders, your parents, and of course, the Holy Ghost to guide you.

See No Evil—
Pornography & Media

My wife has a grandmother we adore. However, as Grandma has gotten older, she has started doing some rather unusual things. If you think you are prone to strange behavior as a teenager, just wait—it only gets worse. (I am hoping that the embarrassment I cause my children when I get older will be sufficient payback for the embarrassment I suffered when they were young.) When we visit Grandma's house, she always invites us to stay for dinner. But the older she has gotten, the more and more interesting those dinners have become (e.g., mold-covered old meatloaf, soda pop that has been on her storage shelf for 20 years, or any number of mouthwatering dishes pulled out of the deep, dark crevices of her fridge or cupboard). One day when we were visiting her house, Grandma was complaining how the people who lived in her basement would throw away perfectly good food. She then went outside and rummaged through their garbage can, picking out some very old ears of corn and other food mixed in with all the other trash in the can. She then brought this food into the house. Everyone was in a bit of shock, as this was *not* a family dining tradition, even for Grandma. She then offered us dinner. Needless to say, my wife graciously declined by saying, "Oh, we couldn't possibly stay for dinner." It isn't hard to understand why dinner at Grandma's was not very tempting that night.

While none of you would probably consider gathering meals by rummaging through someone's garbage, you can, in a very real sense, be filling your minds and spirits with a steady dose of garbage without even realizing you are doing it. Today the media, the Internet, our entertainment, and music are often filled with garbage for the mind and soul, and yet many people rummage through it mindlessly much the way Grandma rummaged through the garbage can that day. Many take in a three-course-a-day, 365-day-a-year, year-after-year diet of this garbage. It is vile and destructive. It makes two-month-old moldy meatloaf look like a tasty banquet. If you were to ingest bad food, you would probably get sick and throw up. But if you take in the spiritual garbage of pornography, vile images, and filthy messages available today, your spirit does not simply vomit that deadly material back up. The garbage we are talking about can be found everywhere you look. It is found in our movies, on the TV, in our magazines, and on the Internet. Once there, it is permanently stored in the computer chip of your brain, available for recall, waiting to flick unbidden across the screen of your mind. Unfortunately, this type of spiritual garbage stays with us. It is far more sickening to the spirit than a simple dinner dug out of a garbage can. Prophets have emphasized the importance of taking in wholesome entertainment. Elder H. Burke Peterson said, "We must not feed ourselves a diet of trash. We become what we think; we think about things we hear and read and see" ("Clean Thoughts, Pure Lives," *Ensign*, Sept. 1984, 72). Elder Joseph B. Wirthlin of the Quorum of the Twelve Apostles said, "Just as we exercise great care about what we take into our bodies through our mouths, we should exert a similar vigilance about what we take into our minds through our eyes and ears" ("Windows of Light and Truth," *Ensign*, Nov. 1995, 77).

It is interesting to me that spiritually sensitive children, whose minds have not been filled with such garbage, seem to know right from wrong instinctively. For example, when my son Jonathan was only about six years old, we went to a local video store to pick up a movie for the family. As we were waiting to check out, I noticed he was looking at something towards the front of the line. There up by the counter were several magazines, one of which just happened to be the *Sports Illustrated* swimsuit edition. You know the issue I'm refer-ring to—the one with some beautiful young lady on the cover who *isn't* covered. I glanced at my son and thought, "You're only six! What in the world could *you* be thinking?" He suddenly pointed right at the magazine, and in a voice loud enough to be heard by all around us, said, "Daddy, that's naughty!" I looked around and thought, *That's my boy!* Thinking about the incident later, I found it interesting that a six-year-old who was not necessarily versed in the ways of the world could tell something was "naughty." I'll make the assumption that you are brighter than my six-year-old was at that tender age.

Today's media, movies, and Internet can all be used for the good of mankind, but too often they serve the pursuits of the father of all lies, Lucifer. Think for a moment how often inappropriate behavior, especially sexual behavior, is shown on television or in the movies to be acceptable. The magazine *U.S. News and World Report* put it this way: "On television, adult virgins are as rare as caribou in Manhattan. Several studies have found that prime-time network shows implicitly condone premarital sex, and air as many as 8 depictions of it for every 1 of sex between married couples" (May 19, 1997, 58). Another survey found that 97 percent of all sexual scenes on daytime soap operas are between unmarried people. Over and over, the message Hollywood wants us to hear is that sex before marriage is acceptable.

But regardless of what the world wants us to believe, the words of the prophets have been consistent and clear. The scriptures condemn such behavior. From Mount Sinai the Lord declared, "Thou shalt not commit adultery" (Ex. 20:14). President Hinckley has also spoken out against those who propagate these lies:

> I encourage you, my dear friends, to speak up for moral standards in a world where filth, sleaze, pornography, and their whole evil brood are sweeping over us as a flood. In the first place, none of us can afford to be partakers of this rubbish. Not one of us, neither I nor any one of you, can become involved with such things as sleazy videotapes, suggestive television programs, debasing movies, sensual magazines, so-called 900 numbers, or the kind of filth that evidently can be picked up now on the Internet. Avoid them like the plague, for they are a serious and deadly disease ("Inspirational Thoughts," *Ensign,* July 1998, 2).

In A.D. 1348, the bubonic plague hit Europe with a vengeance, ravaging the continent for nearly two hundred years. Up to two-thirds of the population of many major European cities died of the plague in the first two years. Most trade came to a halt. People lived in constant fear of dying from the plague and would do almost anything to avoid even the possibility of contact with one who had the dreaded disease, as it meant almost certain death. Unfortunately, today many people are suffering from a similar spiritual plague—the plague of immorality and its acceptance as the norm. We must be on our guard to avoid this plague as literally as the people in Europe avoided the bubonic plague. Remember the words of the Savior, "Fear not them which kill the body, but are not able to kill the soul: but rather fear him which is able to destroy both soul and body in hell" (Matt. 10:28).

We would also do well to apply the warning of Moroni, who saw our day and said, "And again I would exhort you that ye would come unto Christ, and lay hold upon every good gift, and touch not the evil gift, nor the unclean thing" (Moro. 10:30).

Once while teaching an institute class, I asked a young man to give the closing prayer. He looked at me apprehensively and then asked if it would be okay if someone else gave the prayer instead. Immediately after class, he asked if he could speak with me. When we sat down in my office, he explained that he had recently been disfellowshipped from the Church for immorality. He indicated that his problems all started when he begin looking at soft-core pornography—on the Internet, in movies, and in magazines. He said that the more he looked, the more he wanted. Soon soft-core turned to hard-core, and the more he looked, the more he began fantasizing about the things he had seen. It finally led to actions on his part, which led to his being disfellowshipped from the Church. After this conversation, I watched him struggle for years to get rid of this addiction. Finally, he found himself worthy of the full blessings of the Church again. He told me how he constantly had to stay on guard to avoid returning to his previous addiction. He acknowledged how any worldly pleasure associated with this sin was not worth the pain, humiliation, and guilt that went hand in hand with it.

Elder David E. Sorensen commented on the crippling effects such behavior can have on our spiritual senses:

> Pornography destroys self-esteem and weakens self-discipline. . . . Resisting the temptation of today's

electronic media is not easy. It takes focused courage and effort. In the small town where I grew up, one had to drive at least an hour to find trouble. But today on the Internet, trouble is just a few mouse clicks away. To avoid such temptations, be like Captain Moroni of old; set up "fortifications" to strengthen your places of weakness. Instead of building walls of "timbers and dirt" to protect a vulnerable city, build "fortifications" in the form of personal ground rules to protect your priceless virtue. . . . Remember, such "fortifications" are not a sign of weakness. On the contrary, they show strength ("You Can't Pet a Rattlesnake, *Ensign*, May 2001, 41).

This is a disease of epidemic proportions in the world, and unfortunately, also in the Church today. One stake president commented sadly that he had called in five men before he found one worthy to serve in a particular position. The others, he learned, were involved in pornography. Our ability to serve in the Lord's kingdom is weakened (or suspended altogether) when we allow ourselves to get caught up in the filth Satan offers. Not only that, but our relationships with those closest to us suffer, as the following story illustrates.

A young married woman in one of my institute classes came up to me one day and asked if she could talk to me. After class, she told me how she had found her husband on the Internet looking at the most filthy of pictures. When she confronted him, he was offended. He told her he could look at what he liked. She told me how offensive it was to her and how she felt it cheapened her in regards to her inherent beauty as a virtuous daughter of God. With tears rolling down her face, she expressed how much she wished he were a righteous priesthood holder. As she told me this, I was reminded of a quote in the *For the Strength of Youth* pamphlet. It says, "Pornography is a poison that weakens your self-control, changes the way you see others, causes you to lose the guidance of the Spirit, and can even affect your ability to have a normal relationship with your future spouse" (*For the Strength of Youth* [pamphlet, 2001], 19). Sadly, it appeared that not only was pornography affecting this young man individually, but his marriage was being damaged and destroyed as well.

President Hinckley has warned us:

> You live in a world of terrible temptations. Pornography, with its sleazy filth, sweeps over the earth like a horrible, engulfing tide. It is poison. Do not watch it or read it. It will destroy you if you do. It will take from you your self-respect. It will rob you of a sense of the beauties of life. It will tear you down and pull you into a slough of evil thoughts and possibly of evil actions. Stay away from it. Shun it as you would a foul disease, for it is just as deadly. Be virtuous in thought and in deed. God has planted in you, for a purpose, a divine urge which may be easily subverted to evil and destructive ends. . . . The Lord has said, "Let virtue garnish thy thoughts unceasingly (D&C 121:45)" ("Some Thoughts on Temples, Retention of Converts, and Missionary Service," *Ensign*, Nov. 1997, 50).

Can you imagine how much better off we would be if we would heed the words of the prophets? How many individuals have been destroyed by the evil effects of pornography?

The *Ensign* published the story of a man who had a serious battle with pornography for a good part of his life. He indicated that his problems began during his early years and escalated in his adulthood, with devastating effects on his marriage and family life. He said,

> I had an early record that did not indicate problems ahead. I became an Eagle Scout at age 14 and followed that by earning a Duty to God award. Throughout those years I prepared myself to one day serve a mission.
>
> During that time, like most teenagers, I became curious about the opposite sex. By all appearances I continued to be an honorable young man, yet I

ignored cautions from the Spirit against indulging in certain visual stimulations when they came my way.

Like the person who is susceptible to alcoholism, I failed to recognize this as a weakness Satan knew he could exploit. This no doubt set a tone for what was to come later in my life.

I remember attending a regional Explorer camp for 14- to 18-year-olds in my area and watching a movie there. It was rated PG, so I thought it was OK. But it featured a lengthy, inappropriate scene that aroused feelings I had never before experienced. Rather than walk out as I was prompted to do, I cemented that scene in my mind and mulled it over for weeks.

On another occasion, I traveled to a resort community with friends, all from active Church families. Two of them left our room to cruise around and returned with a popular soft-porn magazine. I knew I was standing for the right by refusing to look inside, but my mind was riveted far too long on a series of photos on the cover, and that, too, stayed with me for weeks. . . .

While attending college . . . my roommates and I took in a few of the abundant R-rated movies available in local theaters as well as inappropriate programs on cable television. As priesthood holders, we felt guilty when we failed to live up to our standards—but we didn't change our behavior.

Self-deception became easier as the years went by. I convinced myself that these occasional pursuits were normal male behaviors—simply innocent forays into a little self-indulgence while outwardly remaining active in my Church activities and callings. Looking back, I now realize that I was not slowly casting off sin and advancing line upon line to perfection; rather, I was moving reel upon reel and frame upon frame down the broad path to destruction. . . .

This individual then related how pornography eventually affected his marriage. Fortunately, he was able to tap into the power of the Atonement and repent of his behavior. He continues,

> There is truly one source of light and truth and joy. That source—the Savior—will never leave us, no matter how far we've fallen. He is there to lift us and inspire us, and He holds the only fruit of real worth— that of eternal happiness in His presence. It is ours to grasp if we but repent and obey Him to the end ("Breaking the Chains of Pornography," *Ensign*, Feb. 2001, 55).

Can you see by this story how easy it is to rationalize behavior and come up with excuses to continue in sin? Rationalizations and excuses do not lead us to repentance or change. If you find yourself in a similar pattern, the sooner you have the courage to see your bishop, the better. He will help you get out of this terrible addiction. It will not be easy, since even a slight problem in this area can hinder your sensitivity and ability to recognize the Spirit. Listen carefully to this quote from the *New Era.*

> Pornography first appeals to curiosity. Somehow, just looking doesn't seem all that dangerous. Every one of us has gone into a store just to look—not to buy. But this is a huge store with almost unlimited merchandise. Once we are in the store, the invitations to satisfy our curiosity are endless. And so curiosity is never satisfied.
>
> There are lots of things in life—like rattlesnakes or abandoned mine shafts or drugs—that we may be curious about. But knowing how dangerous they are, we walk away or leave the party or turn off the computer.
>
> Actually with pornography, there is no such thing as just looking. Looking *is* the problem. Viewing pornography triggers sexual feelings. We can easily get hooked on those pleasurable feelings, especially if they

seem to relieve stress or anxiety—and we can start a cycle of addiction just as difficult to break as an addiction to drugs or alcohol ("Danger Ahead! Avoiding Pornography's Trap," *New Era*, Oct. 2002, 34).

Pornography was not invented by sweet little old grandmas who were tired of baking cookies and came up with pornography for the innocent entertainment of their grandchildren. Paul warns of those who are "inventors of evil things" (Romans 1:30). The Doctrine and Covenants warns of "evils and designs which do and will exist in the hearts of conspiring men in the last days" (89:4). Those who produce the filth of pornography are such men. Our leaders have told us, "It is estimated that in recent years Americans alone spent $8–10 billion per year on hard-core pornography—a fortune siphoned away from noble use and diverted to a devilish purpose. . . . One study showed that pornography may have a direct relationship to sex crimes. In the study, 87 percent of convicted molesters of girls and 77 percent of convicted molesters of boys admit to the use of pornography" (Thomas S. Monson, "Pornography, the Deadly Carrier," *Ensign*, July 2001, 2). The link to sex crimes is a frightening reality. We cannot minimize the evil effects of pornography. It is like a poisonous spider that spins its dangerous web around its unsuspecting prey. We have made covenants to stay away from all "unholy and impure practices" (Spencer W. Kimball, *The Miracle of Forgiveness* [1969], 25). Can there be anything more unholy or impure than pornography and its relationship to sex crimes? Let us resolve to keep sacred those covenants and resist even the "appearance of evil."

It is also becoming as spiritually dangerous to take in an evening of television as it is physically dangerous to walk through a minefield in Iraq. The dangers are everywhere you look, and they continue to multiply. This hasn't always been the case, as noted by Elder Boyd K. Packer:

> There are temptations beckoning to you that were not there when we were teenagers. AIDS had not been invented when we were young, and drugs were something a doctor prescribed. We knew about opium

from reading mysteries, but steroids, pills, and crack and all the rest belonged to future imaginations.

Modesty was not mocked then. Morality and courtesy were fostered in books and films as much as their opposites are today. Perversion was not talked about, much less endorsed as a life-style. What was shunned then as pornographic, you see now on prime-time television.

Your challenge is *much* greater than was ours. Few of us would trade places with you. Frankly, we are quite relieved that we are not back where you are. Few of us would be equal to it ("To Young Women and Men," *Ensign*, May 1989, 54).

Notice that President Packer said, "What was shunned then as pornographic, you see now on prime-time television." Want an example? When I was in high school, a new movie came out entitled *Midnight Cowboy.* It was nominated for best picture of the year and won. However, this particularly move was rated X (comparable to today's NC-17 in the United States), and it was the first time in the history of the Academy Awards that an X-rated film had won best picture. A few years later, that same film unedited, uncut was re-released, only it was then rated R. Today, according to Kieth Merrill, a member of the Church and himself an Academy Award winner, if *Midnight Cowboy* were released today, it would probably get a PG-13 rating! Today's PG-13 is equal to the X rating of just a couple of decades ago! How comfortable would you be going to an NC-17 with a date? You probably wouldn't be, yet sometimes we don't scrutinize our choice of entertainment closely enough—we simply rely on someone else's standard to determine ours. It really does not matter if your friends have seen the movie, if the movie is a huge hit, or if it won an Academy Award. The real question should be, "It is a movie a true Latter-day Saint should see?" Ponder the following counsel: "Regardless of what others may do, we should not view or talk about suggestive movies. Shun them as you would the plague" (H. Burke Peterson, "Clean Thoughts, Pure Lives," *Ensign,* Sept. 1984, 71).

I mentioned a recent movie to a class of mine not long ago. Everyone knew that even though it was "only" rated PG-13, it was filled with sexual dialogue and sexual scenes. I normally don't mention a movie by name, but I felt compelled to mention it and condemn it for what it represented. I didn't have to see it to know what its intent was—the few seconds of its trailer told me far more than I needed to know. As I spoke of this movie, I noticed that several of the young men in my class, all returned missionaries, looked at each other and appeared to be ashamed. I couldn't help but wonder why three recently returned missionaries would willingly pay to see a movie that would only hurt their spiritual health. There would be scenes in that movie that would cause unholy, impure thoughts to enter their minds. I wondered what the real cost of the movie was.

Over the years, movies have come out that have been tremendous hits, box-office blowouts, Academy award–winning movies, all accepted with great acclaim by the world. Many even masquerade under a label of PG-13, but they are nonetheless filled with explicit nudity and immorality. I have heard students say this movie or that was all right even with the explicit nudity because it was "art." Have you ever heard the saying, "That bird don't fly"? Well, excuses for "acceptable nudity and immorality" in a movie are just that—excuses. I plead with you to not to go to a movie you know is going to drag you down. Just don't do it! In a world filled with so much filth, you can't afford to pay to ingest more.

I know a young lady who went on a double date to dinner and a movie (how creative!). She hadn't heard anything about the movie, only that it was rated PG-13. Soon after it started, she realized it wasn't up to her standards. She finally leaned over and told her date she didn't really like the movie, so she'd just go out into the foyer and wait. As she was leaving, an older couple was doing the same thing, so she knew at least she wasn't alone. Once in the foyer, she waited and waited and waited and waited. She thought about calling her father to come get her, and after a while, her date appeared and asked, "Do you want to wait in my truck until the movie ends?" (This is not the way to win a young woman's heart, in case you were wondering.) "No," she responded. "I'll just call my dad to come get me." Her date acted a bit put out and said, "Fine, I'll just take you home then." They didn't say a word the entire ride. What do you think his chances are of a second date?

Ratings alone do not always give us a perfect guideline as to what is acceptable and what is not. We have been counseled that R- and NC-17–rated movies are obviously out, but it's important to realize that many PG-13 movies are also not appropriate. Many TV shows are not appropriate to watch. Today more than ever, we must stop and seriously think about what is acceptable. We have been given the Holy Ghost to guide us, and we need to allow His influence to help determine what to watch and what is uplifting. You simply cannot let the world's opinion be the determination of what is acceptable to see.

Hear No Evil—Music

One year while directing a session of EFY, I decided to attend a class being taught by a friend of mine. As I approached, I could hear the youth laughing and singing. I opened the door to hear, "Just sit right back and you'll hear a tale, the tale of a . . ." Can you finish the line? Even though the TV program *Gilligan's Island* is nearly 40 years old, most of today's youth have seen reruns and can sing the song word-for-word. Have you ever noticed how, when put to music, lyrics seem to be easier to recall even though we may not have heard the song for years?

When I was growing up, my older sister would listen to the radio nonstop. It was a time when the "British Invasion" of music was alive and well in the United States. The Beatles were the number-one group in America. They were constantly writing and singing songs that would stay at the top of the charts for weeks on end. What's amazing is that 40 years later, my 18-year-old son can sing most of those same songs word-for-word—and he's probably not the only one. Why is that?

We can pick up the lyrics to a song without even realizing we have. To say, "I don't really pick up on the lyrics; I just like the beat or the melody," is actually a dangerous assumption. The following quote reinforces this:

> You might say, "But I don't listen to the lyrics."
> Research shows that the human brain automatically
> picks up every message within sight or sound. Lyrics

set to music can be especially influencing because they sneak past the screening mechanism of the brain and are stored in the subconscious without your knowledge (Tamara Leatham Bailey and Christie Giles, "The Power of Music," *Liahona*, Mar. 1996, 40).

Music is a powerful force. It can swing our moods to either extreme, it can influence our emotions one way or another, it can affect our actions for good or bad, and it can invite the Spirit or drive Him away. Music can inspire us or tear us down. A song with a catchy beat can help us exercise harder, drive faster (something I can do less often), or work harder. If we can admit that music has a tremendous power, then we certainly must realize that Satan knows these potential effects as well and will use the power of music in every way possible to make inroads into our lives and fulfill *his* sinister desires and purposes. There are also those in the music industry whom Satan has influenced to assist in destroying us spiritually. Gene R. Cook relates a powerful story to illustrate this.

Mr. Jagger and I were on a flight that originated in Mexico and were headed, I believe to either Houston or Dallas. As I sat down in the plane, the seat next to me was empty. Later a man sat down by me. . . . I prayed that the Lord would inspire me in what to say as I talked to this man. After the prayer, I said something like, "My name is Gene Cook, I'm a member of The Church of Jesus Christ of Latter-day Saints. What's your name?" And he said, "My name is Mick Jagger." Not realizing then who he was I said, "Well, I'm glad to meet you, Mick." And then he said, "I said my name is Mick Jagger." . . . And he opened up [a] magazine and pointed to his picture and said, "This is me." . . . I finally said something like, "You know Mick, I have a question for you that I'd like you to answer for me." He said, "Well, I'll be glad to try." Then I said to him, "I have the opportunity to be with young people in many different places

around the world, and some of them have told me
that the kind of music you and others like you sing
has no effect on them, that it's okay, and that it
doesn't affect them adversely in any way. Then other
young people have told me very honestly that your
kind of music has a real effect on them for evil and
that it affects them in a very bad way. You've been in
this business for a long time, Mick. I'd like to know
your opinion. What do you think is the impact of
your music on young people?"

This is a direct quote, brothers and sisters. He
said, "Our music is calculated to drive the kids to
sex." Those were his exact words. I'm sure I had a real
look of shock on my face in receiving such a bold
response. He quickly added, "Well, it's not my fault
what they do. That's up to them. I'm just making a lot
of money.". . . He told me this was a great day for
them because now instead of just having audio where
they could portray some of what they wanted to about
sex and all, they now had videos and could have the
people both hear and see it portrayed. . . . He told me
the importance, in his view, of freeing up the youth.
He felt that they ought to be able to do whatever they
wanted in spite of their parents. . . . He told me that
he was thankful the family, as a entity, was being
destroyed. And I gathered from what he was saying
that he was doing his best to help it along (Gene R.
Cook, address delivered at Ricks College, 1989).

With such bold statements and agendas, it would seem that the
adversary is unleashing his arsenal of spiritually deadly weapons—and
he obviously has plenty of help.

A few months ago, a speaker at the Logan Institute of Religion
made a comment that went something like this: "There is good and
bad in almost all types of music. There is bad rock music; there is
good rock music. There is bad classical music; there is good classical
music. And then there is *bad* country music." He stopped, not able to

bring himself to say, "and there is good country music." The point is, though, that good and bad songs can be found in all types of music—even country music. To categorize different types of music as "good" or "bad" isn't seeing the whole picture. Moral and immoral songs exist in almost every genre of music. What we have to be willing to admit is that there will always be some songs unquestionably unworthy of our time or our money. The Brethren have counseled us:

> You must consider your listening habits thoughtfully and prayerfully. You should be willing to control your listening habits and shun music that is spiritually harmful. Don't listen to music that contains ideas that contradict principles of the gospel. Don't listen to music that promotes Satanism or other evil practices, encourages immorality, uses foul and offensive language, or drives away the Spirit (*For the Strength of Youth* [pamphlet, 1990], 13–14).

I attended a concert of local rock bands that several of the youth in our area were going to be performing in. I went and, unfortunately, was rather taken aback. The music was LOUD, and the lyrics sounded angry and mad at the world. As I watched these youth engage in and enjoy this entertainment, I thought about the possible damage to their sensitive spiritual nerves. I wanted to help them realize that the Spirit does not shout and try to compete for your attention. He does not scream at you when the background noise is loud and deafening. Why do we call the Spirit the still, small voice? Because that's how He speaks to us, and if the outside noises compete for our attention, then those ever-so-quiet promptings will not be felt. Right now is such a critical time to be feeling the Spirit, when you are facing decisions that will affect not only your youth, but quite possibly the rest of your life and eternity. You *must* have the companionship of the Spirit to guide you. Filling your time with music that drives the Spirit away is a very dangerous thing to be doing. I read a story some time ago that illustrates the power and goodness that we can have access to when negative music is shut out of our lives.

The life of 10-year-old Bobby Jenkins seemed to be filled with turmoil. His parents were divorced and his father remarried. Bobby's stepmother was a fine woman, but she just didn't seem to take the place of his real mother.

To make matters worse, his oldest brother joined the Army. That left Bobby at home with his 15-year-old brother Tim, who was his only remaining strand of security.

Then one day, the bottom of Bobby's world dropped out. Tim had drowned in a senseless accident while swimming in a canal.

At the funeral, Bobby seemed to go numb. He had been hurt so many times, he didn't want to feel again.

Except for school and other necessary activities, he hibernated in his room. He turned on the radio to the hardest rock music he could find.

Hour after hour, day after day—even while he slept, the music blared. With its loud and constant rhythm, he didn't have to think or feel. He could separate himself from the world that had hurt him so much.

After many weeks of this, his stepmother couldn't stand it any longer. In the middle of the night, while Bobby was sleeping, she tiptoed into his room and turned off the radio.

The next morning, he poked his head into the kitchen and asked, "Did you turn off my radio last night?"

Expecting the worst, his stepmother gently replied, "Yes, I did."

Much to her surprise Bobby's response was not in anger. Instead, he sat down at the table and quietly shared the feelings of his heart.

"This morning when I woke up, Timmy appeared in my room. He told me he was happy and all was well. He said the Church is true and I should start reading the Book of Mormon. He told me lots of things which really made me happy."

Bobby stopped just long enough to gain his composure, then continued.

"He said that this was the fourth time he had received permission to visit me, but he couldn't come into my room because of the type of music I had on the radio."

With a hint of emotion in his voice, this 10-year-old man said, "Thanks Mom for turning off my radio" (Source unavailable).

Can you imagine his sadness at some future day when he realized what he could have had if he had turned off his music? He would have realized too late that he had the opportunity of a lifetime, but had missed it in the lifetime of the opportunity. He would have realized that his music—something that seemed so harmless—had prevented a beautiful experience from taking place. Luckily, his mother facilitated him being given a great blessing. Reflecting on this experience, can you imagine him wishing for his old music back? I think not. Is there any music that is worth the loss of spiritual blessings? My challenge to you in regards to music is the same one given by Elder Packer almost 30 years ago, when music was more innocent, less violent, less vulgar, and much less dangerous to your soul. It is even more relevant today. He said, "Why not go through your collection? Get rid of the worst of it. Keep just the best of it. Be selective in what you consume and what you produce. It becomes a part of you" ("Inspiring Music—Worthy Thoughts," *Ensign*, Jan. 1974, 27).

My son and I actually had a CD-breaking party one night at our house. It was really rather fun. Let the following list of guidelines help you as you go through your music.

1. How does the music make you feel? Does it make you depressed, frustrated, or angry? Does it drive the Spirit away?

2. Would you feel comfortable reading the lyrics to your family, bishop, or friends? Do the lyrics promote

immorality, Satanism, vulgarity, or use offensive language? Does the message build or tear down gospel teachings?

3. What kind of standards does the performing group promote? How does the group affect the people who listen to their music?

4. Does the CD or jacket have inappropriate material on it? Does it promote inappropriate themes?

There is a definite difference between music that uplifts and music that does not. Take a good, hard look at your music, then have the courage to discard that which does not edify. You will be better prepared to feel the Spirit if you do.

Speak No Evil—Language

I love old musicals, and one of my top-ten favorites would have to be *My Fair Lady*. It is a wonderful show. If you are familiar with it, you probably know the rather arrogant, self-loving Henry Higgins, who believes he can determine a person's origin and even their social status by the way that they speak. He decides to take on the enormous task of reforming and reeducating a street urchin, Eliza Doolittle, and transforming her language in order to dupe the "rich and famous" of the city and pass her off as nobility. While the plot is rather silly, if you stop to think about it there is a bit of truth in Henry's theories. The speech we use does say volumes about our moral character and who we really are. Today, the language of the world is growing more and more vulgar and crude. Even sadder is when members of the Church, who should know better, are found using such language. It is sad to think that as society has become ever more enlightened, our language has become more and more base and vulgar. Elder Dallin H. Oaks related an interesting experience he had in regards to language:

> Recently our family was viewing what was supposed to be a wholesome movie on videotape. Suddenly, one of the actors used a vulgar expression. Embarrassed, we began to smooth this over with our ten-year old daughter. She quickly assured us that we needn't worry because she heard worse than that every day from the boys and girls at her school. . . .

> The nature and extent of profanity and vulgarity in our society is a measure of its deterioration.
>
> I cannot remember when I first heard profane and vulgar expressions in common use around me. I suppose it was from adults in the barnyard or the barracks. Today, our young people hear such expressions from boys and girls in their grade schools, from actors on stage and in the movies, from popular novels, and even from public officials and sports heroes. . . .
>
> For many in our day, the profane has become commonplace and the vulgar has become acceptable. Surely this is one fulfillment of the Book of Mormon prophecy that in the last days, "there shall be great pollutions upon the face of the earth" ("Reverent and Clean," *Ensign,* May 1986, 49).

Notice that Elder Oaks isn't just talking about the "profane," which would consist of at least the words we would consider "profanity" or swear words, but also the "vulgar." Vulgarity includes crude, obscene, or tasteless words, and off-colored jokes or dirty stories—in short, anything beneath the dignity of a true Latter-day Saint. Lewd and offensive language takes sacred things and makes them cheap. The danger in listening to this degrading language is that one day it may become our own, and using such language becomes a terrible habit that, once started, is difficult to break. Words that you may have thought you abandoned long ago can find themselves at your tongue for years to come. President Hinckley told of an experience he had with swearing when he was young boy.

> When I was a small boy in the first grade, I experienced what I thought was a rather tough day at school. I came home, walked in the house, threw my book on the kitchen table, and let forth an expletive that included the name of the Lord. My mother was shocked. She told me quietly, but firmly, how wrong I was. She told me that I could not have words of that

kind coming out of my mouth. She led me by the hand into the bathroom, where she took from the shelf a clean washcloth, put it under the faucet, and then generously coated it with soap. She said, "We'll have to wash out your mouth." She told me to open it, and I did so reluctantly. Then she rubbed the soapy washcloth around my tongue and teeth. I sputtered and fumed and felt like swearing again, but I didn't. I rinsed and rinsed my mouth, but it was a long while before the soapy taste was gone. In fact, whenever I think of that experience, I can still taste the soap. The lesson was worthwhile. I think I can say that I have tried to avoid using the name of the Lord in vain since that day. I am grateful for that lesson ("Take Not the Name of God in Vain," *Ensign*, Nov. 1987, 45).

How many of us need a little "soap" to clean up our language? Can we learn the same lesson President Hinckley learned and avoid using the name of the Lord in vain?

When I was teaching at a seminary in Arizona, my wife attended a football game to support my students on a Friday night when I was out of town. She sat down behind several LDS students who did not recognize her, and she was shocked to hear the language that poured from their mouths when they thought no one other than their friends was listening. It was what my kids used to call *potty language,* which is a term that does not flatter the user. Profanity, it has been said, is the attempt of a feeble brain trying to express itself forcefully. The use of profanity or obscene language does not present us in an intelligent or positive light. In reality, it only shows our weakness. Our language reveals so much about our integrity, honesty, goodness, humility, and our character—or lack of all of those! Think about the men and women you admire greatly. I cannot imagine that they use vile language. President Hinckley reaffirmed this when he said, "Brethren, stay out of the gutter in your conversation. Foul talk defiles the man who speaks it. . . . The man or the boy who must resort to such language immediately says that he is poverty-ridden in his vocabulary.

He does not enjoy sufficient richness of expression to be able to speak effectively without swearing or using foul words" ("Take Not the Name of God in Vain," *Ensign,* Nov. 1987, 44). Elder Robert K. Dellenbach told of an experience from his youth that is worth passing along.

> Making the varsity basketball team in junior high school was probably the most exciting athletic achievement of my life. Just being part of the team and working out with the other players was a thrill.
>
> I still remember what happened during a practice session. One of our teammates missed a pass. Then, a few minutes later, he made another error. This time he swore, and our coach heard him.
>
> Now, Coach Fishburn was the most outstanding man I had ever met. He was bright, and he knew basketball and young men. After the practice, the coach called us together to talk about our practice. And he brought up the subject of profanity. "A good athlete never needs to swear," he said. "Swearing only cheapens the athlete and makes him look weak. Men of greatness have no need for foul language—it only makes them look small in the eyes of other people."
>
> Although my basketball career was brief, Coach Fishburn's words have always stayed with me. "Men [and women] of greatness have no need of foul language." ("Profanity," *New Era,* May 1992, 46).

Have you ever stopped to think what the word *profanity* means? I read an article in the *Ensign* that made me really think about this in a way I had not done before. *Profanity* means outside (*pro*) the temple or shrine (*fanum*). Profane language drags sacred words out and makes them common, making a mockery of holy things (John S. Tanner, "Sin—On the Tips of Our Tongues," *Ensign,* Feb. 1991, 30). Profanity violates what God has said: "That which cometh from above is sacred, and must be spoken with care" (D&C 63:64).

Do you remember on Mount Sinai when the Lord declared, "Put off thy shoes from off thy feet, for the place whereon thou standest is holy ground" (Ex. 3:5)? It was in this sacred setting that Moses was given the name of God, "I AM THAT I AM" (Ex. 3:14), or Jehovah. This name was so sacred that it was almost never pronounced and was hardly ever even written. Then the Mosaic law was given as well as the commandment not to take the name of the Lord in vain. Today, it is probably the most commonly broken commandment given. Have you ever wondered how God must feel when Latter-day Saints speak these words? After all, we have covenanted to bear His name, haven't we? President Stephen L. Richards said, "How regrettable it is that man, seemingly oblivious to this honorable and sacred relationship, should profane his holy name and blaspheme Christ. Do you think that a son can damn his father and love him?" (*Where Is Wisdom?* [1955], 238).

President Kimball related an experience he had when he was being taken out of the operating room after one of the many surgeries he had.

> In the hospital one day I was wheeled out of the operating room by an attendant who stumbled, and there issued from his angry lips vicious cursing with a combination of the names of the Savior. Even half-conscious, I recoiled and implored: "Please! Please! That is my Lord whose names you revile."
>
> There was a deathly silence, then a subdued voice whispered, "I am sorry." He had forgotten for the moment that the Lord had forcefully commanded all his people, "Thou shalt not take the name of the Lord thy God in vain; for the Lord will not hold him guiltless that taketh his name in vain" (Ex. 20:7) ("President Kimball Speaks Out on Profanity," *Ensign*, Feb. 1981, 3).

During a general conference some time ago, President Hinckley read part of a letter asking him to address vulgarity and profanity among our youth. President Hinckley said,

Conversations I have had with school principals and students lead me to the same conclusion—that even among our young people, there is an evil and growing habit of profanity and the use of foul and filthy language.

I do not hesitate to say that it is wrong, seriously wrong, for any young man ordained to the priesthood of God to be guilty of such ("Take Not the Name of God in Vain," *Ensign,* Nov. 1987, 44).

My young friends, shouldn't we be different from the world? Can we all make a solemn vow to watch the words that come forth from our mouths? Our language says volumes about the type of people we are, about our love and respect for our Heavenly Father. Let's promise not to degrade ourselves, others, or God by what we say.

Think No Evil—
Controlling Our Thoughts

Many years ago my wife and I went on a trip that included four days in Egypt. We had the opportunity to travel along the Nile River, which is the lifeblood of the Egyptian people. Without that source of water, they could not survive. As we floated along, I was shocked by what I observed. We came across one person using the bathroom in the river, another bathing in it, a few feet farther ahead dead animals floating around, a few more feet and I saw people dumping their fly-ridden garbage into the Nile, and then—and this is the kicker—a little farther, others *drinking* out of the river or collecting water that was terribly contaminated and polluted. These people were polluting the very water they needed to survive. Of course, none of us were filling our water bottles out of the Nile. I definitely opted to buy bottled water and bathe later! Drinking from the Nile could have made me a lifelong spokesman for Pepto Bismol.

Our minds can be compared to a great reservoir of water. If you think about a sparkling stream as it leaves the mountain, pure and crystal clear, it is much like our minds were when we were born. We entered this life with a crystal-clear mind, unpolluted by the harmful effects of mortality. However, along the way, our mind can become polluted by the things it picks up as it cascades along. A little pornography here, a swear word there, evil thoughts. If we are not careful, our minds can become as filthy and polluted as the Nile river. Cleaning up or decontaminating a water source is a difficult thing to do, just as cleaning up our mind once it is polluted is a difficult task.

The prophet Jacob had to deal with a difficult situation. The men he presided over were breaking the law of chastity, and that, in turn, was breaking the hearts of their women. When he begins the arduous task of addressing this problem, he says, "Know that by the help of the all-powerful Creator . . . I can tell you concerning your thoughts, how that ye are beginning to labor in sin" (Jacob 2:5). Certainly we all know that our thoughts precede our actions, yet do we understand that even *thoughts* can be sinful?

The more we think about something, the more likely we will act on that something. In Proverbs we read, "For as [a man] thinketh in his heart, so is he" (Prov. 23:7). President Kimball strengthened that verse by saying, "As a man thinketh, so *does* he" (*The Miracle of Forgiveness* [1969], 106). Do you see the important change made by President Kimball? We certainly are not going to do something without thinking about it first. Our thoughts *will* precede our actions. However, this process does not stop there. President David O. McKay liked to repeat the following poem about our thoughts and how they affect our actions and eventually all eternity.

> *Sow a thought, reap an act;*
>
> *Sow an act, reap a habit;*
>
> *Sow a habit, reap a character;*
>
> *Sow a character, reap an eternal destiny* (Spencer W. Kimball, *The Miracle of Forgiveness* [1969], 115).

We may want to ask ourselves what eternal destiny we are headed for. Are our thoughts of a celestial, terrestrial, or telestial nature? They may seem like simple, insignificant things, but they do, in a very real sense, determine where we end up. President Thomas S. Monson said the following:

> President David O. McKay advised, "I implore you to think clean thoughts." He then made this significant declaration of truth: "Every action is preceded by a thought. If we want to control our actions, we must

control our thinking." Brethren, fill your minds with good thoughts, and your actions will be proper. May each one of you be able to echo in truth the line from Tennyson spoken by Sir Galahad: "My strength is as the strength of ten, because my heart is pure" (*Familiar Quotations*, p. 647). ("That We May Touch Heaven," *Ensign*, Nov. 1990, 45).

I realize that with all the evil in the world, it can be hard to keep our thoughts clean. Elder Richard G. Scott gives us the following advice. He said, "Some bad thoughts come by themselves. Others come because we invite them by what we look at and listen to. . . . The mind can think of only one thing at a time. Use that fact to crowd out ugly thoughts" ("Making the Right Choices," *Ensign*, Nov. 1994, 37).

Now, "crowding out" ugly thoughts is different from just trying to not think ugly thoughts. To crowd out bad thoughts, you actually have to *replace* them with good thoughts. When a bad thought enters your mind, quickly replace it with a righteous thought. Think about your mom and dad or President Hinckley, the Savior, or your favorite hymn or scripture. You must move your mind elsewhere, and when you do, by all means give yourself a HUGE, double-decker, ice-cream-with-a-cherry-on-top, 2000-calorie pat on the back. Brad Wilcox has given an excellent talk on controlling thoughts, and he stresses the importance of celebrating your private victories. He says:

When you mow the lawn or do homework, people say, "Wonderful!" If you lose twenty pounds, people say, "Outstanding!" When you get your Duty to God or Young Women Recognition award, everyone says, "Excellent!" When I'm really trying to go the extra mile, John Bytheway even says to me, "Thou art cool."

But what happens when we control our thoughts? Do parents say, "Sweetheart, we know that myriad triple X-rated grossities and impurities are spawning in your mind, and you're controlling them. We are so proud of you!" No way! There is no space on the school report card for an A+ in thought control. When I cast out an improper thought, no one really knows except God and me. So it is up to the two of us to throw the party!

He then went on to tell of an experience in an airport where the man next to him had a magazine in plain view that was clearly not even close to the *Ensign* in cleanliness. Brother Wilcox began writing in his journal, saying to himself, "I will not look up. I will not even think about looking up." He said later of the incident, "Now I open my journal to that particular page with a lot of laughs and a great deal of personal pride. It was a victory—a personal victory but nonetheless a victory. I celebrated as if my school had just taken state!"

You and you alone are the master of your mind and thoughts. You and you alone have the power to shape your eternal destiny by shaping your thoughts. Take this simple challenge to keep your thoughts clean. Choose something uplifting to replace bad thoughts when they enter the stage of your mind. Celebrate each private victory when you crowd out improper thoughts. And finally, remember that one day there will be a real celebration when our Heavenly Father will reward you with far more than a personal victory celebration—when He will say to you, "Well done, thou good and faithful servant" (Matt. 25:21).

Whose Side Are We On Anyway?

What is available today as entertainment sometimes seems to be something out of the Cliffs Notes of *A Day in the Life at Sodom and Gomorrah.* Unfortunately, many young people rationalize that they only "occasionally" watch or listen to this kind of entertainment and that "occasional" instances will not affect them. This is a great lie. Listen carefully to this statement by H. Burke Peterson:

> One of the great tragedies is that too many men and boys who hold the priesthood of God are watching and listening to this type of so-called entertainment. . . . They think they are spiritually strong and will be immune to its influence. This trash is nothing more nor less than pornography dressed in one of its many imitation robes of splendor—one of the master counterfeiter's best products. . . .
>
> No man or boy of us here tonight can look at, read about, or listen to such explicit vulgarity, even in its mildest form, without bringing sorrow to a loving God and a terrible injury to one's own spirit. We cannot look at or listen to these unholy depictions in our own living room or wherever they are shown without suffering the consequences—and those consequences are very real.
>
> Brethren, I plead with you to leave it alone. Stay away from any movie, video, publication, or music— *regardless of its rating*—where illicit behavior and

expressions are a part of the action. . . . I know it is hard counsel we give when we say movies that are R-rated, and many with PG-13 ratings, are produced by satanic influences. Our standards should not be dictated by the rating system. I repeat, because of what they *really* represent, these types of movies, music, tapes, etc. serve the purposes of the author of all darkness.

Brethren, let's consider again why we cannot be involved in Satan's program of entertainment and be held guiltless. Why? Because *we are men and boys of the covenant,* and that makes us different from all others. . . . He loves all of his sons, *but those of the covenant have a special responsibility* ("Touch Not the Evil Gift, nor the Unclean Thing," *Ensign,* Nov. 1993, 43).

When my son Joshua was very young, he was notorious for getting into mischief. He and the twins that lived across the backyard loved to do "all manner of iniquity." One day, unknown to their mother, they filled up with water the dirt holes in the field by our house and created their own mud-a-thon. Joshua later came running into the house (nothing but his Superman underwear on), covered from head to toe with mud, with only the whites of his eyes exposed. He exclaimed, "I'm hiding in here!" And he was indeed hiding under all that mud.

There is an analogy in Joshua's statement. If we are not careful, we could find ourselves covered with the mud and filth of pornography and the vile entertainment of today's world, hidden somewhere underneath all the muck and mire. The process of cleansing is not as easy as the backyard hose we used on Joshua that day. Repentance is a difficult process, so heed the danger signs the Spirit points out to you and stay away from the destructive muck. My little experience with my son Joshua has often reminded me of a warning given by Elder Joe J. Christensen: "It is very unreasonable to suppose that exposure to profanity, nudity, sex, and violence has no negative effects on us. We can't roll around in the mud without getting dirty" ("The Savior Is Counting on You," *Ensign*, Nov. 1996, 40).

We really need to be asking ourselves who we are supporting when we select entertainment that is filthy, vile, or inappropriate. If this is the great battle of our day, then whose side are we on? The line dividing both sides is clear—if we are in touch with the Spirit and know the counsel of our leaders. We must decide which side we are going to be fighting on and then stay on that side of the battle regardless of what comes along. We cannot jump sides depending on how badly we want to see a particular movie or how much we like a particular band or what our so-called friends are doing. There is only going to be one winning side, and trust me, you want to be fighting on the winning team. Safety for your soul is found only on one side of the battle line. The Lord's standard does not change and never has. The world's standard continues to allow more and more filth as acceptable, so adhering to the world's standards of acceptability is not going to cut it in the end. Remember Isaiah's warning: "Woe unto them that call evil good, and good evil; that put darkness for light, and light for darkness" (Isa. 5:20). President Gordon B. Hinckley has said:

> Challenging though it may be, there is a way to apply traditional moral principles in our day. For some unknown reason, there is constantly appearing the false rationalization that at one time in the long-ago, virtue was easy and that now it is difficult. I would like to remind any who feel that way that there has never been a time since the Creation when the same forces were not at work that are at work today. The proposal made by Potiphar's wife to Joseph in Egypt is no different from that faced by many men and women and youth in our day.
>
> The influences today may be more apparent and more seductive, but they are no more compelling. One cannot be shielded entirely from these influences. They are all about us. Our culture is saturated with them. But the same kind of self-discipline exercised by

Joseph will yield the same beneficial result. Notwithstanding the so-called "new morality," notwithstanding the much-discussed changes in moral standards, there is no adequate substitute for virtue. God's standards may be challenged everywhere throughout the world, but God has not abrogated his commandments ("With All Thy Getting Get Understanding," *Ensign*, Aug. 1988, 2).

As true Latter-day Saints, each of us should try and live by the article of faith I'm certain we have heard and probably even memorized: "If there is anything virtuous, lovely, or of good report or praiseworthy, we seek after these things."

Modest Is Hottest

Once when I was driving to work at the institute at Utah State University, I happened to see a young lady I had in a class that very semester. As I looked in her direction, I couldn't help but notice what she was wearing. It was almost totally leather, and it was also tight and quite revealing. I couldn't believe it. What was even more unbelievable was the fact that just a couple of hours later that same day, I had her in class—but she had completely changed her clothes! Sitting at institute she was dressed very modestly. I had to wonder if she pulled that little (and I mean *little)* outfit out of her backpack after class and put it back on to greet the world again. It should be obvious that wearing immodest clothing to school simply isn't in keeping with the standards of the Church. But that's not the only place where modesty is required.

There is another phenomenon I've observed in regards to modesty. I like to try and work out several times a week. I go in the morning because I discovered that at the sports facility I frequent, afternoon and evening is filled with the "look at me" crowd. Many of the young ladies dress very inappropriately and wear very little. I find myself wondering what they are thinking—or *not* thinking? Is it acceptable to dress in almost nothing because you might sweat? I appreciate the young people who dress in attire necessary to work out and yet retain their modesty. There is never a circumstance, be it working out, a special dance, or any other special occasion, that warrants dressing immodestly.

When our oldest daughter was a junior, she was asked out to the junior prom. My wife approached me and announced that she had decided I would have the opportunity to go with her to find a dress Sarah could wear. "Why me?" I asked. "What have I done to deserve this sentence?" Anyway, we started the long, torturous task of looking for The Dress. You know, The True and Living Dress, the one she had known in the premortal life. In store after store, I couldn't believe what was being sold under the guise of a *dress*. I had seen more cotton in an aspirin bottle! One store was dedicated entirely to prom dresses, and as I entered with my wife, I realized I was the only person of the male gender in the entire place. Since there wasn't much for a male to do in this store, I started looking for something to read on the table by the couch while my wife started looking for a dress. You can imagine what I found—nothing but girl magazines! Not a sports magazine in the place. I sat down on a couch just as one young lady came out of the dressing rooms and walked toward her mother, who was also waiting on the couches. The daughter's dress left little to the imagination. It was about the size of a dish towel, with a few added sequins. (You know, low in front, low in back, tight all over.) The girl asked her mother, "How do I look?" and I wanted to scream, "You're not planning on wearing that *outside*, are you?" Her mother, however, indicated how beautiful the girl looked in the dress and how it accentuated her sexy figure. She gave it a perfect 10! I, on the other hand, was trying to send mental telepathy messages saying this was not the dress for her. As I sat there, I was amazed at this mother's comments, and I could only imagine this woman kissing her daughter good-bye on prom night in that skimpy little dress and reminding her to stay morally clean. It seemed like such a contradiction. Such immodest dresses put a young man in an uncomfortable position. Where can he possibly put his hands? What types of thoughts do you want him to entertain all evening? Take a hint from this old guy, will you? When selecting a prom dress, pick one with enough material to get the job done, something that honors your Creator. It may be interesting to note here where the word *modesty* comes from.

> The word *modesty* ultimately stems from the Latin term *modus,* meaning "measure." Hence modesty connotes balance, proportion, restraint, and (from the

same root) moderation. Its opposites would be excess, extremity, lack of restraint, outlandishness, intemperateness, immoderation, and so forth. . . . Though it means much more than merely good manners, modesty belongs among the social virtues because it requires sensitivity and tact (John S. Tanner, "To Clothe a Temple," *Ensign*, Aug. 1992, 45).

A couple of years ago, I was directing a session of EFY at BYU. During this session, I got to talk to just the ladies and just the men at different times. Because modesty is such a big deal to me, I spent much of my time talking to the young ladies about this subject. During my talk I mentioned an experience I'd had as a bishop.

A beautiful young lady came in to see me. She had broken the law of chastity a number of times over the years. I tried to help her through repentance. As the interview progressed, she finally looked at me and said, "Why, Bishop, why? Why is it that the only boys who seem to want to date me always want sex?" I looked at her and pondered what I should say. Finally, I said, "Do you really want to know? It might hurt a little."

"Yes, please," she pleaded.

"Okay," I said, "Here's the truth. It's the way you dress. You dress in such a way that the guys looking for sex are attracted to you. The problem is that the good guys, the ones who desire to stay morally clean, wouldn't ask you out. They don't want to tempt themselves." She looked at me with "I can't believe it" eyes. I continued, "If you want to have good young men ask you out, then you must change the way you dress. You must dress modestly."

I related this story to the girls at EFY to emphasize my point of how important it was to dress modestly. Later that week, a young lady came up and handed me a letter. In part, it reads:

I have not been very pure. . . . I am going to be 18 in a month and have been sexually active since I was

15. . . . I started dressing really immodestly and I couldn't figure out why only guys who wanted to have sex wanted to date me. Today when you talked about that, I was just sitting there like "duh." It's like no one had even actually told me, "Hello! The way you dress and act attracts those kinds of guys." Today I wore a tight little black skirt. . . . As soon as I had a chance I went back to my dorm and changed.

Notice how plainly *For the Strength of Youth* puts it:

The way you dress is a reflection of what you are on the inside. Your dress and grooming send messages about you to others. . . . Never lower your dress standards for any occasion. Doing so sends the message that you are using your body to get attention and approval and that modesty is important only when it is convenient (*For the Strength of Youth* [pamphlet, 2001], 14–15).

President Spencer W. Kimball put it this way: "It is a pretty weak girl if she has only her body to attract somebody" (*Teachings of Spencer W. Kimball*, ed. Edward L. Kimball, [1982], 285).

Defining what is or isn't immodest isn't tricky when we know the guidelines that have been set. Again, how grateful I am to belong to a Church that helps us understand what is and isn't appropriate dress.

Immodest clothing includes short shorts and skirts, tight clothing, shirts that do not cover the stomach, and other revealing attire. Young women should wear clothing that covers the shoulder and avoid clothing that is low-cut in the front or the back or revealing in any other manner. Young men should also maintain modesty in their appearance. . . . Someday you will receive your endowment in the temple. Your dress and behavior should help you prepare for that sacred time (*For the Strength of Youth* [pamphlet, 2001] 15–16).

At another EFY, a young man mentioned during testimony meeting how much the young men loved modest women. After he sat down, a young lady got up, looked at the young man, and said, "Do you mean that?" (Not your average testimony.) Again she said, "Do you really mean that the guys would rather have us dress modestly?" The young man looked a little startled, then he said, "Yes, we do." Other young men, of course, chimed in with, "Yes," "You bet," "Of course." The young lady responded, "Okay, then when I get back to the dorms, I'm calling my mom and telling her to get rid of all my immodest clothing, and I'm going to buy modest clothing to replace it."

The next day several of the young ladies were greeted with signs saying, *We love modest women,* and other young men wore shirts saying the same. Later that day, the young ladies greeted the boys with signs saying, *We love gentlemen.* I would love it if every young man and young woman would adhere to those simple statements! If we would only listen to each other!

Just last year, I asked the young men and the young ladies to tell me what they wished they could say to the opposite sex. One of the top answers from the young men to the young ladies was that "Modest is the Hottest!" However, lest the young men think they're off the hook, several young ladies wanted to send the following message as well: "Pull up your pants!"

President Kimball talked about this very thing when he said, "We have only one standard of morality, only one standard of decency, only one standard of modesty, and I hope our men will remember that. There is no reason why a man should go around half dressed either" (*Teachings of Spencer W. Kimball,* ed. Edward L. Kimball, [1982], 286).

A good friend of mine, Brad Wilcox, had an interesting experience. Brad was speaking at a youth conference. He stayed at a member's home and was put in the bedroom of their teenage son who was going to spend the night at a friend's home. As he entered this boy's room, the parents apologized because the walls were covered with pictures of models and actresses wearing "not much more than smiles" (Brad's words). Brad wondered what he could do. Later that night, he found some paper and scissors and cut out circles like the ones coming from a cartoon character. He then taped these circles next to the mouths of the pictures. One read, *I'm going to marry only a returned missionary.* Another one said, *I want to be married in the temple,* and yet another one said, *I am a daughter of my Father in Heaven, who loves me, and I love Him.* When the boy returned to his room the next day, Brad apologized for the words. At first the young man thought it was funny, but after thinking about it, he realized the words and the pictures didn't fit together. The young man also realized that even having those pictures up was a contradiction, since he planned on someday going on a mission and marrying in the temple. As you probably guessed, the posters came tumbling down.

Young men, you really can help if you're willing. Last year at EFY, several girls said to the young men, "If the guys really want *modest girls,* then make sure the *modest girls* are the ones you ask out. It's a bit of a contradiction to say 'modest is hottest' and then turn around and date 'immodest is hottest,' isn't it?"

I was speaking at a fireside for LDS university students about these issues. Afterward, a wonderful young lady came up to me who had dated my son while they were in high school. He is now serving his mission. She stated that she really appreciated going out with my son, as he always made a comment about how modestly she dressed and how much he appreciated that about her. She said how much it meant to her to have her modesty reinforced by someone she dated. Can you imagine if every young man made similar statements to girls who dressed appropriately? More of them would dress modestly, there would be less immorality, less temptation, and ultimately greater righteousness. Young men, you may not realize the influence you can have on young women in the Church and their dress standards. Elder Richard G. Scott has spoken about this very subject:

So many of our own young women sacrifice their God-given endowment of femininity, deep spirituality, and a caring interest in others on the altar of popular, worldly opinion. Young men, let such young women know that you will not seek an eternal companion from those that are overcome by worldly trends. Many dress and act immodestly because they are told that is what you want. In sensitive ways, communicate how distasteful revealing attire is to you, a worthy young man. . . .

Those young women who do embrace conservative dress standards and exhibit the attributes of a devoted Latter-day Saint are often criticized for not being "with it." Encourage them by expressing gratitude for their worthy example. . . .Will you begin a private crusade to help young women understand how precious they are to God and attractive to you as they magnify their feminine traits and divinely given attributes of woman-hood? ("The Sanctity of Womanhood," *Ensign*, May 2000, 36).

Can each of you make a commitment that beginning today, you will dress modestly? No excuses. Your body is a gift from our Heavenly Father. You've heard over and over the scripture in 1 Corinthians 3:16, "Know ye not that ye are the temple of God, and that the Spirit of God dwelleth in you?"

A Heavy Price to Pay—STDs

Several years ago, a young lady, a returned missionary, came into my institute office and asked if she could talk to me. As she sat down and began telling her story, she began to cry.

She told me that as a young lady in her early teens, she hadn't been very active in the Church. She had become involved in serious sin, losing her virginity early. She was sexually active for a couple of years before finally deciding to change. She talked with her bishop, became worthy, eventually went through the temple, and then served a mission. When she spoke to me, she was about 25 years old. She had finally met a wonderful young man, a returned missionary himself. They had talked about marriage, and she was so excited.

At that point in the conversation, I had difficulty understanding why she was telling me all of this information, but what she told me next was totally unexpected. Her problem, she explained, was that sometime during her earlier years when she was sexually active, she had contracted an STD (sexually transmitted disease). If the relationship with the returned missionary continued and the marriage talk became more and more serious, she knew she'd have to tell him that she had an STD. Can you imagine her fear? If they were to marry and then engage in sex, which is acceptable in marriage, he would likely contract this disease, which, for this particular STD, had no cure. She was distraught. While she had totally repented of her sins and had served a worthy mission, there were still ongoing and painful consequences of her past that could not be taken away.

Listen to these recent statistics:

> Kids from all walks of life are having sex at younger
> and younger ages—nearly 1 in 10 reports losing his or
> her virginity before the age of 13. . . . One in four
> sexually active teens will contract a sexually trans-
> mitted disease, or STD. . . . 20 percent of sexually
> active girls 15 to 19 get pregnant each year. . . . Across
> the country, clinicians report rising diagnoses of
> herpes and human papillomavirus, or HPV (which
> can cause genital warts), which are now thought to
> affect 15% of the population. Girls 15 to 19 have
> higher rates of gonorrhea than any other age group.
> One quarter of all new HIV [can cause AIDS] cases
> occur in those under the age of 21 (*U.S. News and
> World Report*, May 27, 2002, 44–45).

Did you catch those statistics? One in four—that's 25 percent—
of sexually active teens has an STD. Even Russian roulette has better
odds! Russian roulette is the stupid game of putting one bullet into a
revolver, spinning the chamber, and then pulling the trigger hoping
that that one bullet doesn't kill you. The odds of losing that game?
One in six. The odds of getting an STD from being sexually active?
One in four.

Several months ago, my family, along with our good friends and
their family, sat down to watch a video. The speaker on it was a
mother and counselor who has spoken all over the world on teen
sexuality. The video, *Sex Has A Price Tag 2000*, is a very disturbing
look at what can happen when a young person takes the chance of
playing around with sex outside of marriage. As a counselor, she
would often have young ladies come in to discuss their worry about
being pregnant. They would take the necessary tests, and if those tests
came back negative (meaning they weren't pregnant) the girls would
breathe a sigh of relief. But then this woman would have to ask them,
"But have you been tested for . . . (she'd list off the many, many

STDs)?" Their reply? "Well, no, but I can't possibly have one of those." Wrong! A young lady has a four times greater chance of contracting an STD than she has of getting pregnant! In the USA in the next 24 hours, 24,000 more teenagers will contract an STD. In fact, the average teen who has an STD doesn't have just one, but 2.4 of them. In 1967, only 1 in 36 teens had an STD; in 1983, it was 1 in 18; today, it's 1 in 4! Taking your chances on contracting a sexually transmitted disease is just foolish. The world's ideas on how to achieve "safe sex" outside of marriage are simply lies, and President Benson had the following to say about such lies:

> Do not be misled by Satan's lies. There is no lasting happiness in immorality. There is no joy to be found in breaking the law of chastity. Just the opposite is true. There may be momentary pleasure. For a time it may seem like everything is wonderful. But quickly the relationship will sour. Guilt and shame set in. We become fearful that our sins will be discovered. We must sneak and hide, lie and cheat. Love begins to die. Bitterness, jealousy, anger, and even hate begin to grow. All of these are the natural results of sin and transgression. On the other hand, when we obey the law of chastity and keep ourselves morally clean, we will experience the blessings of increased love and peace, greater trust and respect for our marital partners, deeper commitment to each other and therefore, a deep and significant sense of joy and happiness (*Brigham Young University 1987–88 Devotional and Fireside Speeches*, [1987–1988], 51).

As the world has become more sexually active, the number of STDs has also increased. In 1950, there were only 5 STDs. However, today there are over 30! Some are bacterial, meaning that with proper medication a person can be cured; others are viral and cannot be cured—the person carries them for the rest of their life. Even of those that can be cured, one of them, if contracted, can begin to destroy a woman's ability to have a child. If she gets it once, she loses 25 percent of her ability to conceive. If she gets it again, it's a 50 percent loss. If she gets it a third time, she will usually become sterile, never able to bear a child!

The most common STD is genital warts, which is the easiest to get. It can lead to cervical cancer, and more women die of this STD (or the cancer that comes as a result) than die of the disease HIV! (The above statistics were cited in the video by Pam Stenzel, *Sex Has A Price Tag 2000*).

A few months ago a young lady entered the emergency room. She didn't know what was wrong, but she knew something was not right. The doctor did an examination, and the results were a complete surprise to her. She had contracted an STD. The girl looked at the nurse who told her this and said, "That's impossible." She went on to explain that even though she had had sex, it was with her boyfriend, who had "promised" her he'd never had sex with anyone else. What a sad story, but it is unfortunately repeated time and time again.

Think about what it says in 2 Nephi 28:21: "And others will he pacify, and lull them away into carnal security, that they will say: All is well in Zion." Can you think of a better example of "carnal security" than the lie of so-called "SAFE SEX?" The only safe sex is complete chastity before marriage and complete fidelity after marriage for both individuals! As members of the Church, be grateful for the clear guidance of the prophets and scriptures in this regard. Can you see the blessing, both physically and spiritually, of keeping this law?

Elder M. Russell Ballard said:

> The youth told me that a clean conscience improves their self-esteem. Their relationships with others are better, and they enjoy a very positive acceptance. In fact, some of them said they have lots more fun because of their high standards. They never have to worry about the dreaded *diseases* that often follow those who transgress the law of chastity ("Purity Precedes Power," *Ensign*, Nov. 1990, 35; emphasis added).

Don't be fooled by the world's standards. If you play around with the fire of sexual impurity, the odds are you will get burned. Statistics do not lie. In fact, they paint a rather frightening picture if you choose to hear. Commit now to be clean. If you have made mistakes, see your bishop and your doctor. Then recommit yourself to live the law of chastity. In today's world, it may well save your spiritual and physical life.

The Road Back—Repentance

Once I was at an EFY in the wonderful land of Alberta, Canada. I had just given my chastity talk the hour before lunch, and as I sat down to eat the cafeteria food (I'd blessed it twice, just in case), a group of young ladies came and sat around my table. It was one of those round tables so everyone could see each other easily. They began asking questions about my talk, and it was great to see how much they wanted to be morally clean. As they asked a few questions, I could sense their genuine desire for answers, and I commented to them, "I'm impressed by your spirits. I am sure you are all striving to live morally clean lives." Well, right across the table from me, one of the young ladies started to cry. I felt so bad. What I had said had apparently touched a very tender nerve with her. The table became very quiet. The girl looked at me and asked if I could talk with her for a minute. The others girls quickly got up from the table and made their way to drop off their trays. This young lady and I went over to a remote part of the cafeteria.

She began telling me about a situation she had allowed herself to get into. There was "this guy," a young man who wasn't a member of the Church, who had started showing her attention at school. He called her up to talk on several occasions, and sometimes he asked if he could come over—but it was always when the rest of her family would be gone from the house. He would come over, and after "talking," he would start kissing her, and well . . . you get the picture. She hadn't gone to the bottom of the ski hill, but she had gone pretty close several times. She looked at me pleadingly and said, "What do I do now?" I could tell she really wanted to know, so I told her, "Well, as I see it, there are at least two things you've got to do. Number one, you've got to see your bishop." She dropped her head and then said, "But, Brother Jacobs, *my dad is my bishop.*" I knew immediately that this would be a difficult step for her, and yet, as a bishop and also a father, I knew in my heart how much her father, as her bishop, would desire to help her. I knew he loved her as his daughter and would do everything possible to get her back on track. "Second," I said, "you've got to stop seeing this guy. He's only using you." She understood and promised she would.

A couple of months later I received a letter from this sweet young lady. She told me that she had, in fact, gotten up the courage to visit with her father, and they were working things out together. In another part of her letter, she related the following: *I talked with [the guy I was having problems with] and told him how I didn't want to see him anymore because I am a Mormon and plan to be married in the temple. He told me it wasn't like I was going to marry him.* (Another example of one classy guy!) She continued: *I told him I didn't believe in sex before marriage and that I was going to marry a member of my church. I told him those were the reasons I didn't want to see him again. He then said in a matter-of-fact way to me, "Well, I have to go now."* She said, *I couldn't believe it. It was like he never cared . . . and I was so worried about telling him.* She went on: *Now I know if you have a goal to marry in the temple you should make sure the guys that you date are members of the Church that have served or want to serve a mission.* I was so excited when I read her letter.

Several years ago, I received a call from LDS Social Services. The woman asked if I had been a bishop. I told her I had, and she replied, "Good, we thought so. I have a special request of you. Would you be willing to come and give a talk to a group of young ladies who find themselves in a hard situation?" She explained that this was a group of young women who were either currently pregnant outside of marriage or who had recently placed their child up for adoption. I asked what topic she wanted me to discuss with them. She explained that many of them were afraid of going to their bishop, and she was hoping I could help them understand why seeing him was necessary to truly repent. They had already had to go through the embarrassment of having to tell their parents, and many didn't want to endure that humiliation again. I accepted the speaking assignment with a great deal of anticipation. What could I say to help them? I prayed to know what the Lord wanted them to hear.

The day finally arrived, and I went to the building where they met. As I entered the room where they were seated, I happened to recognize one of them as a student I'd had a year or two before. She had a hard time looking me in the eye. After an introduction, I stood with a prayer in my heart.

I began by showing a video clip of an experience recorded in John 8. It was the story of the woman who had been caught in adultery. The men were asking the Savior what He would have them do. After all, they reasoned, the law of Moses declared she should be stoned to death. The Savior answered by simply saying, "He that is without sin among you, let him first cast a stone at her" (v. 7). After that, each man "being convicted by their own conscience . . . beginning at the eldest" left her alone (v. 9). The Savior then approached the woman and asked, "Woman, where are those thine accusers? hath no man condemned thee?" (v. 10). The woman replied, "No man, Lord" (v. 11). Notice the compassion of Christ when He said, "Neither do I condemn thee: go, and sin no more" (v. 11). I turned off the video. The room was silent. I told them that I knew—we all knew—their situation, and that I wasn't there to condemn them, but to help them.

As I talked to them, the environment became more comfortable, and I was able to get a smile or two. (I guess I'm just funny to look at.) Finally I asked how many of them had ever driven their father's car. Of course, almost all had. I then discussed how if they wanted to drive his car, they would have to get the keys from him. Sure, they could talk to others about their desire to drive his car, but until they spoke directly to him, no keys meant no driving. I explained that likewise, the Lord has given keys to certain men in the kingdom of God, priesthood keys that authorize these men to help people in the Lord's way when they have been involved in serious transgression. Talking to others about our transgressions just isn't the same in the Lord's eyes, and since the Lord is who we are hopefully seeking forgiveness from, then we must not only talk with Him but also with those whom He has given the keys to preside over us and help us. I told them of my own experience as a bishop, how I truly loved those who had come to talk with me about these difficult issues. I told them of an amazing thing that happened as I had counseled these youth with problems. After a person had resolved their problems, while I would remember some of the transgressions that had been confessed, in most cases *(and I mean this)*, I could not remember who it was that talked with me. Many bishops have had the same experience. I emphasized to them the importance of trusting the Lord's representative and knowing that the point of the repentance process was not to make a person feel unworthy and unloved. When my talk was over, there was a marvelous feeling in the room. I thanked the Lord in my heart for blessing me to help these beautiful daughters of His.

My young friends, if we truly desire to be forgiven, we must follow the guidelines of the Forgiver. Realize that your bishop is under strict mandates not to discuss these problems with anyone. He is only there to help you find your way back, and my experience as a bishop was that often I could help individuals see their own great progress better than they could see it themselves.

A warning: Do not procrastinate resolving sin. Some young people intentionally sin thinking that they can quickly repent. Elder Oaks says such people are simply falling into another one of Lucifer's lies, as found in 2 Nephi 28:8. "And there shall also be many which shall say: Eat, drink, and be merry; nevertheless, fear God—he will justify in committing a little sin; . . . there is no harm in this; and do all these things, for tomorrow we die; and if it so be that we are guilty, God will beat us with a few stripes, and at last we shall be saved in the kingdom of God."

I once had a young lady come into my bishop's office who confessed to having committed a major sin. As we talked, I felt that she was sincere about making things right with the Lord. I outlined what she should do to completely repent, and when her interview was about over, she said, "There's probably one more thing you ought to know. The young man I was involved with just barely entered the mission field." I couldn't believe my ears. During the course of the interview, I had learned that several of her transgressions occurred only a few weeks earlier. I asked her some questions about the young man, and it soon became clear that he had lied to his bishop, lied to his stake president, and then, to compound his sin, went to the temple and took out his own endowments. (For those who haven't been to the temple yet, please understand the seriousness of the covenants you make therein. To knowingly make these covenants without repenting of grievous sin is a mockery to God.) This young man had gone unworthily into the mission field.

I knew I now had a responsibility to the Lord and His Church. The young lady understood and agreed, so later that day, I called the young man's stake president. I asked if he remembered this young man, and he said he did. I then explained what I understood this young man had been involved in. "When did this happen?" he asked. After telling him, it was evident he was not pleased with the young man. "He lied to me," he said. "I was very specific in my questions. There is no way he didn't realize he was lying." Well, after our conversation, the stake president contacted the young man's mission president and explained the situation. The mission president then called the young man in, with an Area Authority present, to talk to him. Can you imagine? The young man was, of course, sent home.

To truly repent of such sins, certain things are required. We've already discussed the requirement to talk with your bishop, but that is not all. Elder Richard G. Scott said, "Do not make the mistake to believe that because you have confessed a serious transgression that you have repented of it. That is an essential step, but it is not all that is required" ("The Power of Righteousness," *Ensign*, Nov. 1998, 69).

There must be more than simply talking to a bishop. One thing that greatly concerned me with many of the youth who came in to repent was their lack of understanding of what it truly meant to do so.

Elder Theodore M. Burton noted what it means to truly repent by examining what true repentance *isn't*. He explained that confessing, suffering, enduring punishment, and feeling remorse may accompany repentance, but shouldn't be confused with repentance itself. He highlighted a scripture in Ezekiel 33:8–11 and explained that the original word used in relation to repentance in the Bible (in Hebrew) was *shube,* meaning to turn back to our Father in Heaven. Furthermore, in Matthew 3:2, the footnote next to the word *repent* clarifies that this word denotes a "change of heart" or a "conversion." Do you understand? Many of the youth I met with mistakenly assumed that talking with their bishop was sufficient repentance, but these scriptures tell us that we must forsake, or, in other words, abandon and renounce those sins. Repentance requires a change of heart towards the sin, as well as a change of direction away from the sin and back towards God.

Repentance may require changing who we hang out with. It may require stopping certain behaviors that have, in the past, led to making serious mistakes. Just as a person who has a problem drinking should probably stay away from a bar or the friends with whom he drinks, likewise, a person who has a problem with pornography would be wise to be very selective in what movies he views, what Internet sites he visits, where he has his computer, or what books he reads, etc. As hard as this may seem to do, if a young couple has had major problems with the law of chastity, often they may actually have to break up in order to make it back on the path.

Before we review the steps of repentance, please remember that repentance is not merely following those steps. Repentance requires real change. While the steps can be a great help in making that change, they are not the change itself.

First, there must be a recognition that we have sinned and that our actions have offended God. Elder Neal A. Maxwell said, "How can we really feel forgiven until we first feel responsible?" ("Lest Ye Be Wearied and Faint in Your Minds," *Ensign*, May 1991, 88). True recognition of unworthiness does not allow for excuses. We must accept that we chose to sin and take responsibility for our actions.

Second, we must feel godly sorrow for our sins. As bishop, I would often have young people come into my office and cry like a baby, telling me how very sorry they were for what they had done. Sometimes, to be honest, it felt like they were merely telling me they'd sinned rather than showing feelings of genuine remorse. It was like they were merely checking off a requirement. If you want to know if your sorrow is godly, a simple test can determine it. Look at 2 Corinthians 7:10, which says, "For godly sorrow worketh repentance to salvation not to be repented of; but the sorrow of the world worketh death." In other words, any sorrow that doesn't lead to repentance, and therefore a change of heart and of action, simply isn't godly. If you can feel a change of heart and see a change of direction, then you know you have godly sorrow. Now, you may still be tempted, but you stay away from the appearance of sin.

A few years ago, a young lady knocked on a bishop's door at the church just prior to the beginning of services, just as he was finishing his PEC meeting. She asked if she could talk with him for a minute, so he dismissed everyone and had the young lady sit down. She then quite matter-of-factly "confessed" a major transgression. He mentioned that church was about to start and suggested that maybe they could meet again afterwards to discuss repentance a little more. The young lady looked somewhat surprised and asked, "Why?" She then continued, "Well, if it would be make *you* feel better."

After church, the bishop asked the young lady, "Why didn't you think we needed to meet after church?"

Her response was rather bold. "Because I've repented," she said.

Taken back, the bishop asked, "What do you mean by that?"

The young lady took out a piece of paper with what he soon realized was a "steps to repentance list" on it. "Because," she began while checking off her list, "I've done this and this and this, and now I've talked to you, so I have repented." This young girl mistakenly thought once she had talked with the bishop, she was somehow done. To her, the repentance process was simply checking steps off a list. *Wrong!* Yes, confession of major sins to a bishop is required, but it certainly isn't complete repentance. Remember, repentance requires a change of heart that includes a change of direction.

Third, you must confess your sin to the Lord and, if the sin is serious enough (as described earlier), to the Lord's appointed servant, the bishop. The confession must cover the magnitude of the sin, not minimize it. If you finally get the courage to see your bishop, make sure you tell him all you should. Otherwise, you'll not feel completely forgiven, and you'll know in your heart, and the Lord will know as well, that you've held back.

Fourth, there must be a forsaking of the sin. We must leave our sins behind us and not turn back to them. Someone once said that some people *claim* they want to leave their sins behind, but they leave a forwarding address. To forsake means to not repeat the sin.

I also believe we must learn better how to yield "to the enticings of the Holy Spirit, and [put] off the natural man" (Mosiah 3:19). Be willing to listen to and obey the Spirit. We all have had experiences when we knew we shouldn't do a certain thing or go to a certain place or see a certain thing, and yet we did it anyway. The more we refuse to listen to the Spirit, the more the sin will become a part of us, and the more difficult it becomes to yield to what is right. To yield to the Spirit means to "give way." (The traffic yield sign in England actually reads "Give way.") To "give way" in repentance means to give up what one may naturally desire to do and instead do what the Spirit prompts. Truly repentant people are willing to do anything necessary to feel the cleansing power of forgiveness. This concept of yielding is such an important step because the repentance process can require us to prove, over time, that we have changed and are willing to listen and follow the Spirit.

After we have truly repented, unparalleled blessings come from our Father in Heaven, one of which is peace of mind and heart. When I was a seminary teacher, a young lady came to talk with me. She was very beautiful and well mannered. When she was in the ninth grade, a senior guy had started to take her out. Unfortunately, she had not kept the "Don't date until you're 16" rule or the double-date rule. The young man was not a member of the Church, but he was popular at school. He took advantage of her, and she lost her virtue. She cried and cried as she told me all of this. I got her to see her bishop, and over time I could tell she was making the necessary changes, changes that included whom she dated, the friends she hung around with, and the rules she followed. She began to read her scriptures and pray like she never had before. I was able to watch her progress from year to year. She graduated from high school and seminary, and about two years later, I was thrilled to receive a letter from her. I opened it and there before my eyes was a picture of this beautiful young lady standing next to a rather good-looking young man, a returned missionary. They were to be sealed in a temple for time and all eternity. She was glowing with the light of the Savior in her eyes. She had personally tasted of the miracle of forgiveness.

That miracle can be yours and mine. Some may say, "But if I've lost my virtue I can't get it back!" Perhaps the technical definition of virginity can't be restored, but I know that the Lord can restore virtue! I promise that the Lord desires you to come unto Him and be perfected in Him. He promises He can change your heart and forgive you. I know that our Savior is willing to forgive us, to cleanse us, and to make us whole again. While you cannot change your past, with true repentance you can become clean and prepare for a future worthy of all the Lord's choicest blessings. One of my favorite verses is found in the first chapter of Isaiah. Israel had been in grievous sin, yet the Lord still declares: "Come now, and let us reason together, saith the Lord: though your sins be as scarlet, they shall be as white as snow; though they be red like crimson, they shall be as wool" (v. 18). What a promise! What a reality!

Worthy of the One You Marry

Most of you have heard the statement, "Don't give up what you want most for what you want at the moment." If we are truly trying to earn a place in our Father's kingdom, there are certain things we want most: a clear conscience, a temple wedding, a righteous eternal companion, etc. If we keep those goals foremost in our minds, when temptation comes, we will be able to withstand the "fiery darts of the adversary" because our goals are clear. The blessings of reading our scriptures, praying each day, and serving others cannot be overestimated, as they keep us on the path toward our ultimate goals.

The great blessings of being "chaste while being chased" are many and tremendous. They include living with a clear conscience, holding your head up, knowing that your life is not sullied by such sins. They also include knowing that through the great miracle of forgiveness, you can be clean every whit.

So the question is, what do you need to do right now, while these all-important goals seem to be so far down the road? Have you ever stopped to wonder what your future eternal mate is doing right now, this very minute? Have you ever wondered what standards he or she is keeping, the kind of people he or she is dating, the type of life he or she is living? Have you ever prayed for your future mate to live a worthy life? Have you prayed that you will have the strength to be worthy of your future mate?

A seminary teacher had a boy in his class who bragged about all the girls he kissed. In fact, one day he commented that he could not even count how many girls he had kissed, but his record was six in one day before 2:00 P.M. The teacher then asked what type of girl he would want to marry. This young man mentioned—by name—a wonderful, spiritual girl, who had set a goal to only kiss a young man when she knew he was the one she would marry. The next day, the teacher grabbed this young man and said to him, "Guess what, your kissing record has been broken."

"By who?" he said.

"Your future wife," the teacher responded. The young man stated that the teacher did not know who he was going to marry. Then the teacher said, "You are right, but I am telling you who you deserve." Ouch! But this is true. This young man apparently didn't understand that he attracts the type of person he is, not the person he *isn't*. Good young ladies look for and desire good young men who have kept themselves clean—and vice versa. The Doctrine and Covenants explains this beautifully. It says, "For intelligence cleaveth unto intelligence; . . . virtue loveth virtue; light cleaveth unto light" (D&C 88:40).

I mentioned my daughter Sarah earlier. As I've written this book, she has come into my mind again and again. I love her so deeply as my daughter. No, she is not perfect, but she is strong and true to the gospel, especially to these principles.

As I was worrying about Sarah beginning to date, I finally decided that I wanted to be her first date. So I called her up on the phone from work and asked her out on a date for her sixteenth birthday. (She couldn't say no or she wouldn't have keys to the car.) The night of our "hot" date arrived. I left through the back door and came around to the front and rang the doorbell to pick her up. I had a bouquet of roses for her. We went to a fancy restaurant and had dinner, and then I presented her with a CTR ring. I told her that I hoped that she would wear it to remind her always of the choices she had to make to one day marry the wonderful man of her dreams. I told her that every young man after our date had to respect and honor her as much as I had on that night.

Young men, do you realize that every time you ask a young woman out, she is some parent's most cherished and valued blessing in the whole world? You have an obligation to honor and respect young women, to treat them the same as you will one day pray a future young man will treat your own precious daughter.

Why talk about my daughter so much? Two days from my writing this page, my little princess, all grown up now, will enter the Logan Temple to be married for time and all eternity to a worthy, wonderful priesthood holder. I have watched her grow from a beautiful baby to a beautiful young woman who, because of her obedience to the principles of the gospel, will be sealed to the man of her dreams. She reminds me of the famous verses in Proverbs that proclaim, "Who can find a virtuous woman? for her price is far above rubies. The heart of her husband doth safely trust in her. . . . Strength and honour are her clothing; and she shall rejoice in time to come. . . . Her children arise up, and call her blessed; her husband also, and he praiseth her" (Prov. 31:10–11, 25, 28).

Young men, your focus right now should be on what you can do to make yourself the man that the young woman of your dreams will desire to love and marry. You can reserve your very best for her. Listen to President Hinckley's counsel:

> The girl you marry will take a terrible chance on you. . . .
>
> You have a tremendous obligation toward the girl you marry. Perhaps you are not thinking much of that now. But the time isn't far away when you will think of it, and now is the time to prepare for that most important day of your lives when you take unto yourself a wife and companion equal with you before the Lord. . . .
>
> The girl you marry can expect you to come to the marriage altar absolutely clean. She can expect you to be a young man of virtue. . . .
>
> She will wish to be married to someone who loves her, who trusts her, who walks beside her, who is her very best friend and companion. . . . She will wish to be married to someone who loves the Lord and seeks to do His will. . . .

As I have said, you will wish to be married in one place and one place only. . . . You cannot give to your companion a greater gift than that of marriage in God's holy house. . . .

Choose carefully and wisely. The girl you marry will be yours forever. You will love her and she will love you through thick and thin, through sunshine and storm. She will become the mother of your children. . . .

How precious a thing is a baby. How wonderful a thing is a child. What a marvelous thing is a family. Live worthy of becoming a father of whom your wife and children will be proud.

And so, my dear young men, you may not think seriously about it now. But the time will come when you will fall in love. It will occupy all of your thoughts and be the stuff of which your dreams are made. Make yourself worthy of the loveliest girl in all the world. . . .

Young men, now is the time to prepare for the future. And in that future for most of you is a beautiful young woman whose greatest desire is to bond with you in a relationship that is eternal and everlasting.

You will know no greater happiness than that found in your home. . . .

God bless you, my dear young men. I could wish for you nothing more wonderful than the love, the absolute total love, of a companion of whom you are proud and worthy in every respect. This choice will be the most important of all the choices you make in your life. I pray that heaven may smile upon you in the choice you make, that you may be guided, that you may live without regret ("Living Worthy of the Girl You Will Someday Marry," *Ensign*, May 1998, 49).

Young people, the Lord loves you more than you can imagine. His guidelines about life and chastity aren't given with the desire to ruin your weekend or your teenage years, but rather to keep you happy, to keep you safe, and to keep you pure from the sins of this world. I hope this little book has given hope, guidance, courage to change, an understanding of the great miracle of forgiveness, and in the end, a resolve to keep the laws of the Lord.

My desire and prayer for you is to be truly happy, and to find real joy in this life and eternal life in the world to come. If we will all follow the words of the living prophets and the scriptures, we will never look back with regret. Sister Sheri L. Dew said, "Choose carefully who you listen to, and then listen. Choose carefully who you will follow, and then follow. . . . If we don't listen to the prophet, we might as well not have one" ("Living on the Lord's Side of the Line," in *Speeches of the Year, 2000* [2001], 176).

I love this verse of scripture: "Let virtue garnish thy thoughts unceasingly; then shall thy confidence wax strong in the presence of God. . . . The Holy Ghost shall be thy constant companion, . . . thy dominion shall be an everlasting dominion, and . . . it shall flow unto thee forever and ever" (D&C 121:45–46).

Such is the promise of those who are chaste while being chased.

ABOUT THE AUTHOR

Curtis Jacobs has taught in the Church Educational System for over twenty years and currently teaches at the Orem LDS Institute. He is a popular speaker at BYU Education Week, Especially for Youth, and Know Your Religion programs. Curtis and his wife, Jolene, are the parents of four children.